© 1991 **SINGAPORE YOUTH FOR CHRIST**

RAFFLES CITY P.O. BOX 1017

SINGAPORE 9117

PRINTED BY CHIN LONG PRINTING SERVICE

ISBN 981-00-3003-7

To all ·
the "young"
who have
found the
Lord Jesus

Thy hand, O God

ORIGINAL · EDITION

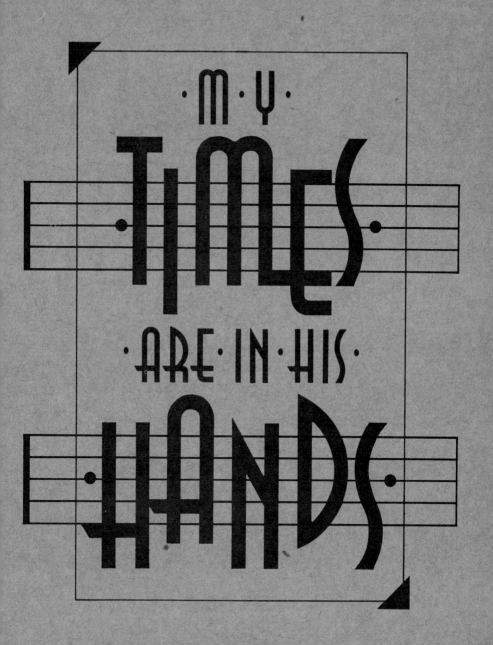

·M·Y·
TIMES
·ARE·IN·HIS·
HANDS

A BIOGRAPHY OF
DR. BENJAMIN CHEW

ACKNOWLEDGEMENTS

This book would not be possible but for the help received from the following persons: Mr Albert Lee for initiating the project; Mr Charlie Lee and Mrs Yong Soo Li for carrying out extensive interviews with Dr Chew and others; Miss Sayyidah Talib for researching and writing the book; Dr William Fry of Taylor University, Indiana for editing; Professor Ernest Chew and Mrs Hu Kee Cheng for reading the first draft and offering helpful suggestions; Mr Ting Pin Sing and Miss Chua Guat Kheng for proofreading the manuscript; Mr Eric Mak for the cover design and layout; Mr Winson Tan for photographic work; and all else who contributed in one way or another. It is most certainly not one person's achievement.

Several books have been written in recent years bemoaning the fact that today's youth have no heroes. Christian youth in Singapore and through their witness, many others across the world do have an authentic role model.

This book tells the story of a life lived in obedience to the heavenly Father. Dr Benjamin Chew was a name that came up frequently in meetings of Youth For Christ leadership in the US and across the world. Naturally I wondered who this man was whose influence and reputation touched so many, so deeply. As a result of many visits to Singapore and numerous opportunities to be near Dr Chew and those of this "Timothys" who lead in various capacities in both church work and in Youth For Christ, I have a sense of the contribution that one man can have for Christ and His Kingdom.

This book will help to fill in the gaps for many who have not had day-to-day contact, but who have wondered at a distance about the source of Dr Chew's influence. In this book you will meet a multifaceted man with a variety of talents, from poetry to music, to business, healing, teaching, and preaching. Most of all you will meet Christ as He incarnates Himself in one life. All who read this account, but especially young people, will be inspired to "give of their best to the Master."

Dr Chew does not claim perfection, indeed, he would be embarrassed with the word. What we do see is a convincing display of the fruit of the Spirit that is available to all youth who will dare to follow in the same footsteps.

Jay Kesler
President
Taylor University, Indiana

Dr Jay Kesler is President of **Taylor University,** Indiana which is one of America's oldest Christian liberal arts colleges. He has written and compiled many books, including "Parents and Teenagers," "Being Holy, Being Human." Articles by him have appeared in numerous evangelical publications. He speaks on "Family Forum," a daily five-minute broadcast aired on over 250 stations across USA. He serves on the Board of Directors and Board of Advisors of numerous Christian organisations including Youth For Christ International and Youth For Christ USA.

Details of the photographs and illustrations can be found on p 158.

Singapore. Boat Quay.

1

2

PROLOGUE

Grow old along with me!

The best is yet to be,

The last of life,

for which the first was made:

Our times are in His hand

Who saith "A whole I planned,

"Youth shows but half;

trust God: see all nor be afraid! "

4

He fixed thee mid this dance
Of plastic circumstance,
This Present, thou, forsooth,
would fain arrest:
Machinery just meant
To give thy soul its bent,
Try thee and turn thee forth,
sufficiently impressed.

What though the earlier grooves

Which ran the laughing loves

Around the base,

no longer pause and press?

What though, about thy rim,

Scull-things in order grim

Grow out, in graver mood,

obey the sterner stress?

7

Look not thou down but up!

To uses of a cup,

The festal board,

lamp's flash and trumpet's peal,

The new mine's foaming flow

The Master's lips a-glow!

Thou, heaven's consummate cup,

what need'st thou with earth's wheel?

9

11

But I need, now as then,

Thee, God, who mouldest men;

And since, not even while the whirl was worst,

Did I, – to the wheel of life

With shapes and colours rife,

Bound dizzily, – mistake my end,

to slake Thy thirst:

11

So, take and use Thy work:

Amend what flaws may lurk,

What strain o' the stuff,

what warpings past the aim!

My times be in Thy hand!

Perfect the cup as planned!

Let age approve of youth,

and death complete the same!

(Extracted from Robert Browning's poem, "Rabbi ben Ezra").

13

O perfect Love,

all human thought

transcending,

Lowly we kneel

in prayer

before Thy throne,

That theirs may be

the love which knows

no ending,

Whom Thou forevermore

dost join in one.

O Perfect Love

ot a day passes when he is not reading the Bible or making music. And today was no exception. The afternoon found Dr Chew at his piano playing Handel's "The Harmonious Blacksmith" whilst Mrs Chew dealt with the plumber in the kitchen.

Benjamin and Hock Neo have been married for almost sixty years. The memory of their golden anniversary was captured in the camera's eye and placed behind glass and a wooden frame on one wall of their living room. Another photograph on the adjacent wall preserved that moment in history when their lives were first joined together. But these cannot contain the substance of those years.

Geylang, Lorong 24 was where they first met. Ben and his extended family consisting of little sister Ada, Mum and Dad, Grandpa and Grandma, and a host of aunts and uncles left their family home in Malacca and came to live in Singapore in 1910. Ben was only about three then. They settled in house number 432 which accommodated the large household comfortably. 432 was a spacious bungalow with six bedrooms upstairs. The space downstairs was taken up by the kitchen, dining room and sitting room. The verandah overlooking the kitchen became Ben's room. It was here that love for Hock Neo first blossomed in his heart.

" 	ow beautiful she is," he thought to himself as he quietly admired the dainty kebaya-clad figure at house 440 across the narrow "lorong". One would expect of most nine-year-old girls that they would be busy playing "masak-masak ," enacting the woman's role in their private world. But Oh Hock Neo had more serious preoccupations. She would often be seen carrying her baby sister in her arms while keeping an eye on another sister playing beside her. The care and kindness with which she carried out her responsibilities was carefully noted by her secret admirer. Ben, who was three days younger than her, was very impressed by her gentle and mature ways.

Ever since that day she occupied a special place in his heart which has never been filled by any other. How they were brought together was undeniably an act of providence, and the Methodist Mission could boast of a part in it.

15

Singapore. Suburban. Police Station.

Sowing in the morning,

sowing seeds of kindness,

Sowing in the noontide

and the dewy eve;

Waiting for the harvest

and the time of reaping,

We shall come rejoicing,

bringing in the sheaves.

Bringing In The Sheaves

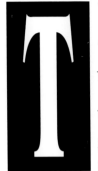he Shellabears,
who were missionaries
with the Methodist Mission,
arrived at their new post, Malacca,
in February 1904. They eventually settled in
Bandar Hilir from which they got to know the Malays and the
Straits-born Chinese. Mr William Shellabear, an ardent Malay
scholar, devoted most of his time to the translation of the
Bible into Malay while his wife, Emma, visited homes in the
neighbourhood with the intention of starting a girls' school. A
second generation missionary graphically recorded her efforts
as follows:

"Up and down the ancient, narrow streets she went, where
doors were less than twenty feet apart. Nearly all the houses
were the same — a front room with a huge altar covered with
red and gold hangings, one or two ornate blackwood chairs, a
pair of huge vases and large wall hangings. Behind that
another room, behind that a court with a steep staircase to
the upper floor. Behind that more rooms and more courts
until at last from the kitchen court a door opened into a small
plot of ground where were kept a few chickens and ducks.
The only windows in such a house were the two in the front
room, for on either side were other houses to form a solid

row. Along the aristocratic Heeren Street Mrs Shellabear courageously knocked at every door, and, though she received very little response, her hope never faltered."[1]

Then she came to 122 Heeren Street, the house of Tan Keong Keng, the eldest son of the late Tan Choon Bock — one of the founders of the Straits Steamship Company and the richest man in Malacca. In the early 1860's Tan Keong Keng had the good fortune of travelling in England and the United States, and resided in the States for five to six years. He was a broad-minded man and one of the earliest among the Straits Chinese to accept western ideas. Thus he was more than happy not only to have his five daughters educated but to have a school started at his home.

His daughters were equally delighted with the idea. Malacca was ultra-conservative and no respectable Chinese woman could be seen on the street. Even to go a few doors a woman had to get into a closed-up palanquin-like hammock called "redi." It was suspended from a pole carried by two men. A little peep-hole provided the occupant with her only window to the outside world. Is it any wonder that the Tan girls gladly welcomed Mrs Shellabear and her school?

Thus the Methodist Girls' School was born with the Tans and their relatives as the first students and Tan Keong Keng's eldest daughter Siok Kim, otherwise known as "Besar" (meaning "big;" the eldest was given the nickname, just as the youngest was called "kechik" which

[1] Means, Nathalie Tom, p 85.

means "small") as the first teacher. Mrs Shellabear would go three times a week to help Siok Kim in school. At other times she would be busy operating her "schoolbus," a pony and gharry bought by husband William, which would shuttle the children to and from home and school. All the shutters had to be closed lest the little girls be seen, and so in darkness and suffocating heat the trip was made each day behind the little pony.[2] But it was a trip worth making because slowly but surely, with every trip, the shutters of their minds were being lifted, dispelling the darkness of ignorance, and reviving and nourishing their spirit.

Siok Kim was more privileged than most of the Chinese girls in Malacca. She was taught English a little over a year before she started teaching at the school. Prior to that she had learnt about Christ from Miss Pugh of the British Foreign Bible Society who ran a Sunday School at the Tans' home. She was thus the fruit of what was at the time a very rare set of circumstances which served to lead her to make a very important decision in December 1904 that determined the direction her life was to take. Mrs Shellabear recorded the happy event in her diary: "William has had the great honour of baptising the first Chinese woman convert in Singapore (Nonya Sin Neo) and now he has baptised the first one in Malacca, Miss Tan Siok Kim."[3]

2 Means, Nathalie Tom, p 86.
3 Means, Nathalie Tom, p 87.

His oath, His covenant

His blood,

Support me in

the whelming flood;

In ev'ry high

and stormy gale,

My anchor holds

within the veil.

On Christ the solid rock

I stand;

All other ground

is sinking sand,

All other ground

is sinking sand.

The Solid Rock

he Tan brothers were furious. Their brother, a Christian! Unheard of! They would not tolerate this.

What's more, he had unashamedly declared his household to be Christian and sealed his decision by destroying the family altar. A definite disgrace to the family name. Zealous over her new-found faith, Siok Kim, with the help of her missionary friends, managed to bring the rest of the household over to Christianity. Only one brother held firmly to his Buddhist beliefs.

Drastic action was taken by Keong Keng's kin. He was disowned and all his assets were transferred to one of his brothers. In spite of such fierce opposition from his relatives, he resolutely stood his ground.

The time came when Keong Keng had to perform one of his duties as a good father which was to see his daughters happily married and well provided for. The age at which the Chinese girl was married was either eighteen or nineteen, but it was common among the wealthier families to marry their daughters two or three years earlier. And Siok Kim was already close to twenty years of age. But good Christian husbands were hard to come by in Malacca. They were a rarity.

At the advice of the local missionaries, Keong Keng journeyed to Singapore in search of suitable matches for his five daughters. They suggested Oldham Hall, the Methodist boarding school for the sons of Chinese from around Singapore, and home to many of their missionary teachers.

Five fine young men passed Mr Tan's strict scrutiny and an exchange of photographs was duly performed. Having accomplished his mission and armed with the black and white portraits of his prospective sons-in-law, Keong Keng returned to his family a satisfied man.

Siok Kim was matched with Chew Cheng Yong. She never met him in the flesh until her wedding day. They made each other's acquaintance by correspondence. The closest they could get to being with one another was by matching the words on the letters with the frozen image on the cardboard paper. Being the eldest daughter, she was the first to be married. The rest of the sisters followed suit in subsequent years.

The pressure from disapproving relatives did not wane. Finally, in 1909, the Tan Keong Keng family left their home for many years in Heeren Street, and began life anew in Singapore.

The odds against living next to a Christian Chinese family in the early 1900's in Singapore were great, but when the patriarch Tan Keong Keng built a house at Geylang Lorong 24 for his extended family, who should live next door in that dominantly Buddhist neighbourhood but a Presbyterian Straits Chinese family — the Ohs. The invisible hand of God was at work in bringing them together.

On 25 November 1915, at their residence in Geylang Road, Tan Keong Keng left to be with his Lord.

The tall trees

in the greenwood,

The meadows

where we play,

The rushes

by the water

We gather

every day.

All things bright

and beautiful,

All creatures

great and small,

All things wise

and wonderful,

The Lord God

made them all.

All Things Bright And Beautiful

The Chews lost their firstborn, Joseph

when he was a few months old. So it was a joyous day for Cheng Yong and Siok Kim and their extended family when on 11 October 1907 Benjamin Chew was born. For the next three years, until sister Ada arrived, Ben was the favoured child of the household.

When the family moved to Singapore, Ben was already an active three-year-old lad. He soon got to know his peers in the new neighbourhood. The Ohs' eldest boy, Thiam Hock, became one of his most faithful playmates. Right from the start Ben and his band were united in their quest for sport and adventure. The compounds of their homes could not contain them and they sought a larger playground.

The wider neighbourhood beckoned with promises of fun and excitement. It did not take them long to discover the big drain at Lorong 24, the prawn fisheries at the Geylang mudflats, the moat at Fort Road or the "padang" next to the Oh house. Even a near drowning incident at the Joo Chiat seashore left no mark on Ben's spirit and he resumed his ventures with undiminished fervour. Peirce Reservoir's forbidden waters was their "private swimming pool" courtesy of their friend, Benjamin Sheares' father, who was employed by the Municipality to take charge of the reservoir.

Perhaps equally strong as his love of adventure was his insatiable thirst for knowledge. "Mum, why did the birds just now fly straight and then suddenly go in a circle? Mum, why...?" In the bedroom, at the hall, at the verandah and even outside the bathroom door his incessant queries would follow Mum. He desperately needed to understand things and sought for answers relentlessly and with a great sense of urgency.

Fortunate for him, Mum was a former school teacher. Besides receiving a general education, she had training in music as well. She was one of the very few women in Singapore who could play both the piano and the violin. It was she who imparted the love for music to Ben. She taught him everything — reading, drawing, writing and, most important of all, the Bible. The countless hours spent in faithfully teaching the truths of God and her efforts in making the lessons interesting and simple enough for his young mind were to bear fruit later in his life.

Apart from being Ben's teacher, Mum was also the disciplinarian. Dad had assigned her this duty as he felt he had a heavy hand. She cut a different picture from the caricature of a disciplinarian as the strict-eyed, tight-lipped, matronly figure, "rotan" in hand, muscles tense and alert, ready to strike the frightened bottoms of wayward children.

When Ben resorted to telling lies to get out of a scrape, Dad decided that he had to be punished and left Mum to the job. First, she gently but firmly explained to him, "I have to punish you to make you realise no liar can ever get into heaven." Then she reluctantly picked up the cane and hit seven-year-old Ben's palm twice with tears running down her face. It was those tears and not the cane that made a lasting impression in young Ben's mind.

But it goes against

the way I am,

To put my

human nature down

And let the Spirit

take control,

Of all I do;

'Cause when

those trials come

My human nature

shouts the thing to do,

And God's soft prompting

Can be easily ignored.

Thank You Lord

en's bright and knowledgeable.

There's no reason why he shouldn't be in school. In fact, Cheng Yong, we're opening a branch school in Geylang. It's so near home. Ben could simply walk across. I could make sure that he goes on to the main school in Fort Canning," said Robert Hanam as he looked fondly at Ben.

Robert, an Anglo-Chinese School teacher, was a church fellow-elder and good friend of the Chews. He had a special liking for Ben and was keen to see him enter school. Subsequently, at the age of nine, Ben entered the Geylang branch of the Anglo-Chinese School — a small single-storey building by the roadside (the present site of the Geylang Post Office). The school had about 70 students, 4 teachers and a tall and an austere Eurasian, Miss Smith, as principal.

Ben was placed in the second standard; and when it soon became obvious that he was ahead of everyone, he was promoted to the third. It did not take long for him to feel that he was a cut above everyone else. He saw himself as their superior in intelligence and character. The praises of doting aunties at home served to further boost his pride. It is a sure saying that pride comes before a fall. In Ben's case it soon came in the shape of two canings by the stern Miss Smith for not heeding her warning to improve his handwriting. His pride was hurt more deeply so because he was expecting her praise for scoring full marks at the geography test!

After three months and still nursing his hurt pride at the seeming injustice, he was promoted to standard four at the main school in Coleman Street, and six months later to standard five. By now he was a confirmed proud little "Pharisee" — nobody got "G's"(the best grade) the way he did, and surely no one memorised as many scripture verses as he, and none but he could boast of being the nephew of Goh Hood Keng, the school supervisor!

At the end of the school year the report cards were handed out. The air was charged with expectancy. Each student almost jumped out of his seat when his name was called; the report card was opened ever so gently as if afraid that an unfriendly phantom might leap out; and the eyes would reluctantly focus in on the handwritten words and figures — the final pronouncement on each one's academic achievement and conduct for the year.

As for Ben, there was no doubt in his mind that he would do well; with him it was a matter of how many "G's" he could get. But even he did not expect the three "G's" that greeted him when he opened his report card. With an air of triumph he thought, "I would surely get a double promotion." Thus, he was walking on air when Uncle Goh Hood Keng, the supervisor, called him to his office. "He wants to tell me the good news of my double promotion," thought Ben. He was quite unprepared for what ensued.

"Ben," started Uncle Goh in his gentle tone and sympathetic countenance, "I'm going to tell you something that will disappoint you. You have done extremely well and normally I should send you to standard seven." He paused and chose his words very carefully before proceeding. "You are ten now and if I were to double promote you, you'll be only 14 when you get through your Senior Cambridge — too young to go anywhere. It's not good for you to be idle while waiting to qualify for college. So I made a decision not to double promote you but to send you to standard six."

Ben stood rooted to the ground. Uncle Goh's final statement fell on him like a ton of bricks. From that day on he lost his former enthusiasm for schoolwork and adopted a careless attitude — one which persisted for the rest of his school days. It was a good thing for him that knowledge advanced at a slower pace in those days. That, together with his mum's prodding , saw him through. He still managed to do well and even obtained several distinctions for his Senior Examination in 1922 which earned him a scholarship for college.

However, his experiences at school were not all negative; there were many memorable moments, like the evening his mathematics teacher, Mr Hoisington, let them gaze at the

stars through his telescope at his home at Mount Sophia. Or
the hilarious moments when they would imitate Mr Thomas's
South Indian accent; this history teacher of theirs would say
"Rooshian" instead of "Russian," or "buttery" instead of
"battery." He lived next door to Ben and would often invite
him over for a game of badminton. Or the time he played the
female role of Portia when they staged Shakespeare's
"Merchant Of Venice"; being the shortest boy in class, he was
most suited for the role!

But the incident that had the deepest and most lasting
effect on his person took place one morning in 1920 at the
school chapel in Coleman Street (now Canning Rise).

16

When I survey

the wondrous cross,

On which the Prince

of Glory died,

My richest gain

I count but loss,

And pour contempt

on all my pride.

When I Survey
The Wondrous Cross

Blessed is the man that walketh not in the counsel of the ungodly, nor standeth in the way of

sinners, nor sitteth in the seat of the scornful ...''.
The voice of Rev Dr Stanley Jones rang in the hall as he read
from the Scriptures. There wasn't the usual chatter in the
back rows; the six-foot tall evangelist held the students
spellbound during his message.

Ben, the Chapel pianist for that morning, stepped down
from the platform and headed for the front row. As he sat
there he arrogantly thought to himself, "It's certainly not for
me." He had memorised every verse of the psalm. But as Dr
Jones began to expound on the verses he was brought face
to face with his true character. In a flash he saw that he
belonged to the same camp as the scornful, the sinful and
the ungodly. A sense of horror swept over him and he "heard"
a voice rebuke him: " You're not a Christian. You're not my
child. You cannot be a Christian because you sit in the seat of
the scornful. You're proud. You look down on others. You
don't really care for them."

The words broke him. Once proud and self-righteous, now
he could only plead for mercy. As tears rolled down his

cheeks, he prayed, "Lord, please forgive me. Cleanse me. Come into my heart and change me." Right away he was filled with a sense of peace and the assurance that he was now a child of God.

As he walked down Coleman Street after school, he was in a state of euphoria. The cockroaches scurried away to escape his quick steps. A rat would hurriedly cross his path and rush into the nearest drain; the only ones that stayed put were the dead ones. Litter was everywhere. But in Ben's eyes that day there could not have been a more beautiful street anywhere else in the world!

He could hardly wait to get home and break the good news to his mum. As he took the mosquito bus home, he was oblivious to the other passengers, the cries of the street pedlars, and the miscellaneous traffic. The minute he reached home he rushed into the house and called for his mum. "Mum, I'm a Christian. I'm a Christian!" Mum grabbed him and as she hugged him tears welled up in her eyes and she gave thanks to God for what He had done. The many hours spent in teaching him the scriptures were not in vain. God in His special way had brought the lessons home to Ben, in a way that she never could.

One evening, in the quiet of the verandah, he sat by his desk and wrote these words in the front page of his Bible: "Jesus loves me, for the Bible tells me so" and "More about Jesus would I know, more of His love to others show." These were lines from the choruses and hymns Mum taught him, but for the first time the words held a depth of meaning. The Bible became a living book to Ben; it was God's authoritative word to him which spells out the way that brings life. He had always known the Bible as a good book. Now he tasted "that the Lord is good" as he kept on reading and studying the good Book.

Give of your best

to the Master

Give of the strength

of your youth;

Throw your souls

fresh glowing ardour

Into the battle

for Truth.

Jesus has set

the example

Dauntless was He

young and brave

Give Him your

loyal devotion

Give Him the best

that you have.

Give Of Your Best To The Master

The Brethren church at Bras Basah

Road was experiencing a revival among their young people. Ben was among more than twenty young people who were baptised that day.

"Benjamin Chew, I baptise you in the name of the Father and of the Son and of the Holy Ghost." Mr James Teskey, the church missionary's booming voice still echoed in the church hall as he plunged fourteen-year-old Ben backwards into the baptism pool. As Ben ran in the rain to the house behind to get changed out of his wet clothes, the incident of his conversion a year ago came to mind. That was a marvellous day indeed and today's occasion stood pale in comparison.

There was a sense of camaraderie in the changing room as he was joined by friends Thiam Hock and Benjamin Sheares who were also baptised that day. They had grown up together in the Sunday School. The two Bens had by then already developed the habit of having morning and evening devotions. One of their Sunday School teachers, Miss Maxwell, had introduced them several years ago to Scripture Union notes which she received from London. Every Sunday she would give them the portions for the week. Their Sunday

School teachers were personal friends; their relationship with their students extended beyond the Sunday lessons.

Mr James Teskey had been instrumental in inculcating in the young people the need to reach out and for total surrender of their lives to God. As a boy, Ben felt that being a missionary was the highest calling and the most noble vocation. Although at the time it was a rather romantic idea of missions that captivated his young mind, later as a medical student he understood it in the proper spirit of sacrifice.

Ben's father no doubt had a part to play in stirring up his interest in missions. Dad had a love for missions. He supported the work of the China Inland Mission. He had two large volumes of George Mueller's faith mission in Ashley Downs, the orphanages in Bristol, which Ben would pore over. He was enthralled by the way God would provide for the needs of this great man of faith as he sought to look after the children who had lost their parents during the dreadful London plague.

Dad had always been active in Christian work. Before Ben was born, he and Uncle Hood Keng were fellow-workers at the Malay service of the Middle Road Church (the present Kampong Kapor Methodist Church). He later resigned his office and resumed work in the Anglo-Chinese School but continued as an earnest worker in the church. He sat on the Mission Worker's Provident Fund Committee. Even after he resigned from teaching to become secretary of Kim Seng Land Co Ltd, he continued to be an active lay person. Encouraged by the Methodist Bishop, he joined the Brethren Church to strengthen their arm and became an elder of the church. Dad was certainly a busy man; but, he had undoubtedly left an indelible mark on young Ben's spiritual life.

Uncle Goh Hood Keng, a teacher-pastor who combined his school job with that of the pastorate, was very much respected and loved by Ben. He was the first Straits-born Chinese to enter the local pastorate of the Methodist Church. The eldest son of a staunch Buddhist, he was brought up in a home where regular times for prayer were strictly observed. Hood Keng said of himself:

"At the age of seven I was put in the Anglo-Chinese School for my education, and while I was there I came under Christian influence and teaching. Being of a religious turn of mind, I naturally was anxious to know what this new religion was that the missionaries had come all the way from America to offer to the people here. As I made a study of the New Testament, and listened to the preaching of the Gospel at the chapel exercises every morning in the school, I was gradually being convinced of the truth of Christianity. I found that what I needed most was some power outside of myself that could come into my heart and enable me to live the right kind of life."[4]

Hood Keng rose to become the first minister of the Baba

4 Song Ong Siang, p 442.

Church (later called the Straits Chinese Church) where he served from 1912 to 1951, the longest pastoral appointment in Methodist history. He was an outstanding evangelist. When he preached at a school chapel service, 20 to 30 young people would come to the Lord.

He married Ben's second aunt and lived for a time at the Geylang house. Ben would very often sneak into his room where Uncle Hood Keng would talk to him about the Lord and the Bible.

Ben was surrounded by many models of fine Christian men and women at home, in school, and at church. Each had in a small or big way left their mark upon his life.

17

Bras Basah Road,
Singapore

He leadeth me,

O blessed thought!

O words of heavenly

comfort fraught!

Whate'er I do,

where e'er I be,

Still 'tis God's hand

that leadeth me.

He leadeth me,

He leadeth me;

By His own hand

He leadeth me;

His faithful follower

I would be,

For by His hand

He leadeth me.

He Leadeth Me

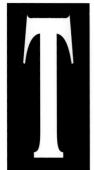o Ben, the choice of a vocation was a question of doing good. A good way to help other people was to take care of their physical well-being. Motivated by this desire to serve others and not because of the prestige attached to the profession, Ben chose to be trained to become a doctor.

There were not many options for higher education in Singapore in 1923. The only college available then was the King Edward VII College of Medicine. Ben spent some months at Raffles School to study some more Science whilst waiting for his Senior Cambridge results in preparation for his future medical studies. So did his friend Benjamin Sheares.

After the results were out, armed with a joint letter from the principal of Raffles School, Mr D A Bishop, both boys went to see the College principal. The two hopeful applicants stood up straight in front of Dr MacAlister's desk waiting to be interviewed; Ben, an inch short of being five feet tall, and Benjamin, only two inches taller than he. In their crisp shirts and shorts they looked like mere boys. Dr MacAlister looked up at them, pushed his spectacles down, gazed at their young faces with his piercing eyes, and in a deep voice said,"You have come to enter the college, have you?" His statement brought a prompt reply from the boys: "Yes, Sir." He would hardly have been surprised if they had saluted him and clicked their heels.

Ben then gave him the letter from Mr Bishop. After reading it, Dr MacAlister looked at them again and asked, "Do you know what is inside the letter?" at which they chorused, "No, Sir." He continued, "This letter is not a recommendation. Your principal desires you to stay on in the school so that you can both become Queen's Scholars and you can have your education overseas." Disappointment and resentment was written all over Ben's face as he turned to look at Benjamin. Having ascertained their interest in the course, the benevolent principal asked, "Do you really want to enter the college?"

The full weight of their desire and enthusiasm gave a charge to the same two words like never before: "Yes, Sir!". They need not say more. With a twinkle in his eye and a half-suppressed smile, he dropped the letter into the waste-paper basket. This simple gesture caused the young faces to instantly brighten up as their hearts welled up with hope. He said, "Well, you shall enter the college." A smile escaped from their lips and quickly grew into a grin and in perfect unison they gave a final resounding, "Thank you, Sir!" — an audible full-stop which neatly and resolutely ended that day's interview.

For the first time that year, the medical course was extended from five to six years. In the additional year, which was termed the pre-medical year, students were taught the Basic Sciences — Biology, Chemistry and Physics — before proceeding to medical studies proper. The academic year began in June and was divided into three terms each of three months duration. The Trinity term extended from June to August, the Michaelmas term from October to December and the Lent term from January to March. Ben joined the College in the Trinity term of 1923. He was awarded an exhibition of the value of twenty dollars a month. As an exhibitioner he was exempted from payment of tuition and examination fees.

Ben and his friends arrived at College that first morning of the new academic year looking well-groomed in their smartly pressed shirts and long pants having been earlier told by the other students, "No short pants!". Little did they realise that they were to be victims of the light-hearted but rough initiation practices of their Seniors. The Senior students mercilessly ragged their new college mates. They forced them to swallow unreasonable doses of calomel, a purgative, and the evil-tasting castor oil; and rubbed into their hair iodoform, a foul-smelling antiseptic. Fortunately for Ben, his small build evoked their sympathy and they spared him the full impact of their harmful schemes.

Ben and his friends survived the ragging; but, they were a

pitiful sight indeed as they staggered down from College that
day to catch the bus home. Their bodies exuded a repulsive
odour which the other passengers in the mosquito bus could
barely tolerate, even though they pinched their noses
throughout the journey! Ragging was not altogether a bad
experience because it did help them to get to know their
Seniors, some of whom later became their good friends.

It was a chastened group of Juniors that went for their first
Science lesson the next morning. Classes were held at the
College premises at Sepoy Lines. Some of the buildings were
those of the former Female Lunatic Asylum whilst others had
been built earlier to serve the College. It was in Ben's first
year that the foundation stone of the new College was laid.
The impressive three-storey building with its elegant columns
and relief sculpture was completed two years later. It
provided ample accommodation not only for the ordinary
undergraduate classes but also for advanced study and
research. Ben and his college mates had the privilege of
enjoying the new facilities and the fully equipped
departments during their last three years at college. They also
had the great privilege of having very distinguished professors
and lecturers.

Professor Kay Mouat, the Professor of Physiology was
probably the most popular amongst students. An Oxford
blue, he cut an impressive figure with his six-foot tall, broad
frame, his elegantly trimmed moustache and goatee and his

unique attire. There was nothing extraordinary about his smart white suit except for one item — a brightly coloured bow. Red, blue, and even orange were just some of the colours from his multi-hued collection. Every so often during his lectures, he would pause a moment, reach out to touch his bow, and as though assured, resume teaching.

One day, he drove up to College as usual in his noisy two-seater Trojan car; but when he stepped into class, it was obvious to all that he had forgotten to sport his bow. Nobody could pay attention to what he was teaching; everyone held their breath, waiting for him to reach out for the non-existent bow. Sure enough, with clockwork precision the critical moment arrived. Astonishment amounting to shock was written all over his face when he realised his bow was missing, and his face turned red within seconds. The class could hardly contain themselves; they burst out in hysterical laughter and was joined promptly by the Professor himself. These lighter moments aside, Ben and his classmates benefitted much from his lectures which were very advanced. It was some years later, as a young doctor, that Ben understood the true value of Professor Mouat's physiology lectures which at the time he found to be profound, far ahead of textbooks.

Ben's second and third years at College were devoted to the study of anatomy and physiology, acquiring a knowledge of the normal structure and function of the human body.

During his fourth year, he entered the wards and received instruction in case-taking and elementary clinical medicine and surgery. He also attended courses in systematic medicine, pharmacology and pharmacy and commenced the study of pathology and bacteriology. In his fifth year he studied surgery, midwifery, medical jurisprudence and public health whilst continuing the study of pathology and attendance at hospital clinics. That year was significant in Ben's academic career because it was then that he experienced his first failure. He failed his pathology paper in his fifth professional examination. It was not that his answers lacked substance; on the contrary, he was penalised for writing much more than what was required. It was a painful way to learn the importance of accuracy. He had been taking things fairly easy, putting in only a few hours of study each night; but for the next six months he worked like never before and passed with distinction when he took the fifth and final year examinations together.

The six years of medical training ended on a high note for Ben. When he and his classmates were anxiously waiting for the results of the final examinations, Professor Kay Mouat himself came out of the office, looked quickly around and when he found Ben, exclaimed, "Congratulations! You have done extremely well!" Ben looked at him in doubt and surprise and could only respond, "Thank you, Sir. Thank you." He had come out top.

There was no fanfare or ceremony when Ben and six others graduated in March 1929. Mortar boards were unknown to them then, graduation robes were unheard of, and "convocation ceremony" was not in their vocabulary. They received the Diploma of Licentiate in Medicine and Surgery(LMS) through the post or by hand. The knowledge that they made it through the training was reward enough for them.

Faith of our fathers,

we will love

Both friend and foe

in all our strife,

And preach Thee, too,

as love knows how

By kindly words

and virtuous life:

Faith of our fathers,

holy faith,

We will be true

to Thee till death.

Faith Of Our Fathers

Professor C J Smith, a Professor of Surgery at the College during her earlier years, once commented,

"The students here, compared with those at home, were too gentle and timid and their manners were too good for medical students." He would never have predicted the student strike which took place in 1924, one which aroused considerable public interest. In some ways, it was an example of student unity — a credit to the success of the two-year-old Medical College Union.

It was a rebellion against the strict regime of Mr F G Street, the Hostel Janitor, the immediate cause of which was a new rule he introduced against which the hostelites protested violently. Dr MacAlister held a dialogue with the students when the matter came to his attention. They perceived him to be unsympathetic toward their cause. Having thus failed to gain his support, they decided to stage a strike; they forsook their classes and spent three glorious weeks instead at a seaside bungalow near Joo Chiat Road. A few of them stayed away because they were refused permission by their parents to participate in the strike. The whole affair resulted in a court inquiry and penalties were subsequently imposed on erring students.

The only student who was expelled was Wijesekara, a final year student from Ceylon. Ben and some of his other collegemates did not want to see his talent and training go to waste, so they raised funds to send him to Edinburgh to complete his training. Such was the deep concern the students had for one another. He eventually became the top man in the Ceylon Medical Service. At the end of it all Dr MacAlister met them and expressed his regret over all that happened. "I would have given my right arm for it not to have happened," he lamented. Thus ended the one and only strike in the history of the College and college life returned to normal.

Ben did not suffer too heavy a penalty; he had to forfeit three weeks of his exhibition money but was allowed to take his examinations. Though he was not a hostelite, he had taken part in the protest because he was moved by a deep sense of justice. That was a testimony to the esprit de corps among the college students. Their loyalty to the College continued even after graduation. They would return to the College to get to know the undergraduates and often to pit their skills against them in chess, badminton or tennis. Ben continued to support these activities after he graduated by donating the Challenge Cup for the Graduate-Undergraduate Badminton Series.

Within the larger student body was an inner circle of Christian students in which this sense of fellowship also prevailed. Although there were no formal Christian groups at College, the Christian students knew one another and met often for mutual encouragement. They sought opportunities to share their faith with their friends on a personal basis, and interested friends would be invited to church. They would also invite their non-Christian friends to attend gospel meetings, and several of them turned to the Lord.

R elationships with other students had not always been warm and friendly where Ben was concerned. He had several unpleasant encounters with students who had anti-Christian sentiments. When it became known that he was a Christian, some of them would deliberately poke fun at him. They would tell vulgar jokes in his presence, and would tease him by calling him "Reverend" because of his relationship to Rev Goh Hood Keng. They made his life miserable in his first two years at College. However, it gave him plenty of opportunities to exercise patience and to keep a curb on his anger. He had a fiery temper; but ever since he had become a Christian, he had kept up the practice of depending on God's help whenever he was tempted on occasions to react in anger. They finally stopped harassing him, especially because he refused to be provoked.

But as he sat by the beach with the sea breeze blowing across his face and looking out at the vast blue sea, all these past events were far from his mind. Ben had escaped all the graduation celebrations to recuperate from the stress of several months of intensive study. He went to his favourite refuge, his father's seaside bungalow at Padang Terbakar in Changi. He was determined to have a month's self-imposed holiday, but that was not to be his privilege.

18

The Beach, Singapore

Teach me Thy patience;

still with Thee

In closer, dearer

company,

In work that keeps

faith sweet and strong,

In trust that triumphs

over wrong.

O Master, Let Me Walk With Thee

Ben's holiday
ended prematurely
when he received a government
order requesting him to report for
work to the Principal Civil Medical Officer(PCMO).
Very reluctantly, he reported to Mr Hoops, the PCMO, a portly
man with a kind face, who proceeded to present to him his
options for service. Because he preferred a medical position,
Ben had no choice but to opt for the only vacancy which was
at Penang General Hospital. That was where he began life as
Dr Benjamin Chew.

He had never been away from the family before. That,
coupled with the fact that he was only 21 years old, was
enough reason for his family to question his going. But it was
an order. So he had to go. Just before he left, he was
engaged to Hock Neo. It was a poignant moment as they
waved each other goodbye at the train station. As the train
picked up speed, the picture of his beloved fiancee waving at
him grew fainter. "I'll be back within the year to marry her,"
he silently told himself. When distance finally cut her off from
view, he turned his attention to the little packet she had
hurriedly pressed into his hand before he got on the train. He
carefully unwrapped the packet and there lay before him a

neat bundle of dollar notes. He counted five hundred dollars in all — a handsome sum in those days. Dr Chew's heart was gently warmed as he reflected on Hock Neo's kindness and generosity. He was sure that she had emptied her savings for his sake. She could not have known then that her gift helped to sustain her fiance for the next three months when his salary of two hundred and fifty dollars per month was delayed due to administrative red tape. It assured him that he could trust God to provide for him and it reminded him that there was one who loved him dearly back home.

He may have left his family behind, but there was a second family which warmly received him into their fold. It was the family of Christ in the form of a small group of believers who met in a church near the seafront along Farquhar Road. The church missionary, Mr Ashdown, looked after Dr Chew just like he would his own son. He very quickly, quite naturally and almost instinctively involved himself in the life of the church: he played the organ during meetings, taught in the Sunday School, and helped out in the youth group. He made many good friends there. Still, he missed his family, and especially Hock Neo. After nine months, he wanted very much to go home. He mentioned to the CMO that the PCMO had promised to get him back to Singapore within a year. Not wanting to lose his favourite and competent anaesthetist, the CMO refused to let him leave.

Dr Chew got to thinking and decided to request a mutual

transfer with his former collegemate Dr Lye Hong Cheong, a Penangite who was serving in Singapore. So he asked for all the leave that he was entitled to and together with Dr Lye who was working in Singapore presented their application to the PCMO. Mindful of his earlier promise to Dr Chew, the PCMO decided to allow the transfer. So he wrote a note to the Penang CMO explaining the new arrangement. That aroused the anger of the CMO and he made life miserable for his unfortunate new assistant. Dr Lye could only tolerate his bad humour for one and a half years after which he resigned to become an estate doctor.

As for Dr Chew, the first thing he did was to marry Hock Neo, his childhood sweetheart of fourteen years, on 29 November 1930. He was then appointed the officer in charge of the outpatient clinic at Joo Chiat. The clinic was opened in 1927 for the care of mothers and infants in one of the most densely populated rural areas. A few months later, he was posted to the Surgery Department of the Singapore General Hospital. The four-year-old General Hospital at Sepoy Lines was the largest in Singapore with an eight-hundred bed capacity.

He worked under Mr K Black, the Chief Surgeon, a brilliant surgeon who could perform an appendicitis operation in six minutes. Dr Chew had high regard for him. But an unfortunate incident took place one night which caused him to lose his respect for the man. That evening a patient was brought in with a ruptured spleen. He contacted Mr Black rightaway at the Singapore Club. "Oh yes, I'll be coming. I'll be coming," he assured him. An hour went by. No sign of Mr Black. Dr Chew and some nurses had set the patient up for surgery. But the surgeon was not in sight. He called him again and received the same assurance. He did finally come about three hours later and rushed on with the operation. Later on, after being transferred to the ward, the patient died. When Dr Chew discovered the death, he was very angry and openly said to Mr Black: "Do you know that if you had come earlier this man would never have died."

He had an acute sense of morality and decided to leave the Surgery Department. The very next morning he requested a transfer to the Medical Department. "I don't like Surgery," he told the CMO, Dr MacGregor.

Dr MacGregor probed further, "Is it because you don't like surgery, or is it because you don't like the surgeon?"

"I can't answer you that," was his brisk response.

"I think you have answered me," replied the perceptive CMO. He was sympathetic to Dr Chew and did his best to arrange for a transfer. Within a month or two, he was finally doing what he liked best — Medicine.

I yield my powers

to Thy command,

To Thee I consecrate

my days;

Perpetual blessings

from Thy hand

Demand perpetual songs

of praise.

My God, how endless

is Thy love!

Thy gifts are

ev'ry evening new;

And morning mercies

from above

Gently distill

like early dew.

My God, How Endless Is Thy Love

After a short stint as an Assistant Medical Officer in the Surgery Department, Dr Chew was

transferred to the Medical Department where he practised General Medicine. He worked under Dr V H Norris, one of two locals who had been promoted to the position of Medical Officer of the Malayan Medical Service. Dr MacGregor, the CMO, approached Ben about starting a clinical laboratory at the hospital. He believed it was a good thing for doctors to do their own clinical work in the laboratory. They could then examine blood specimens or body fluids for themselves. So it was that Dr Chew set up Singapore General Hospital's first clinical laboratory in 1931. It was situated in the Lower Block near the wards. He was put in charge and he had some assistants to help him. He would take blood specimens from the various wards and would examine them himself. He became known for his special skill in taking blood specimens from children. Instead of sending a dresser, he would sometimes walk as far as the Upper Block to take blood specimens from first class and second class patients. He was allowed to examine the cases and had access to the doctor's notes. As a result of his laboratory work, he was able to gather a large amount of case studies.

An interesting incident took place one evening in connection with the laboratory. Dr Chew was on duty when a man was brought in with a painful swelling in his groin. He recognised it at once as a "bubo." His bloodshot eyes and sickly appearance were symptoms consistent with the dreaded plague. The fact that he was a seaman added further weight to Dr Chew's suspicion since there had been no incident of Bubonic plague in Singapore. He acted fast. First, he performed a bubo-puncture. With the help of the other doctor on duty, he stained the bubo-specimen and examined it under the microscope. Sure enough, it was the plague — the first case ever in the colony. They immediately called up Middleton Hospital which was a "specialised" hospital for the treatment of infectious diseases and transferred the case.

The next morning, the Straits Times announced Singapore's first case of Bubonic plague. In their enthusiasm Dr Chew and his colleague had forgotten to report the previous evening's happenings to the CMO. He came in with the morning's papers in his hand and exclaimed, "Chew, what's this here?" The urgency of the whole matter had to be explained. That was but one incident that confirmed the value of the clinical laboratory. The laboratory was also of tremendous help for the purpose of blood typing for blood transfusions.

Apart from laboratory work, Dr Chew had his medical

duties to perform. He started working in the third class wards where the greatest number of cases were found. Maternal and infant mortality rates were high and the death rate averaged 23% per year. The principal diseases then were malaria, tuberculosis(TB), typhoid and enteric fevers, beri-beri and venereal diseases and other infections. This scenario posed a great challenge to the medical staff. Their task was made all the more difficult as they did not have the vast array of specific medication available to doctors today. Antibiotics were not available; sulphonamide, an inferior substitute for antibiotics, was only available in 1940. Penicillin came into use in 1946.

As House Physician, he was also responsible for the cases directly under the Physician. Any calls regarding these cases would be directed to him and not to the Physician. So he ended up with quite a number of first and second class cases. As a House Physician he would have to be on call all the time. Sometimes, the doctor on duty might call him. At other times the patient, especially if he were a first class case, would ask for him. He was House Physician under Drs Norris, Landor and Professors R B Hawes and G A Ransome. Professor Hawes, the Professor of Medicine at the Medical College from 1927 to 1938, was an inspiring teacher who stimulated a good deal of original applied and academic research in Clinical Medicine. He was understanding and considerate toward Dr Chew.

Working as House Physician to Professor Ransome was certainly an interesting experience. Ransome was a perfect example of the absentminded but gifted Professor. There was once when he kept the Governor of one of the nearby Colonies waiting three days for treatment while he was engrossed with another case, a coolie in the third class ward. Another time, the Professor, in a panic, reported to the police that his car was stolen. The police arrived only to find it at the back of the Upper Block. He had parked there that evening instead of at his regular parking space at the front. On yet another occasion, he kept his wife waiting at home because he got carried away in his conversation with Dr Chew at a hospital visit. It was about nine pm when he suddenly exclaimed, "My wife! I've got to take her out to dinner." Despite these idiosyncrasies, he was an excellent diagnostician. Dr Chew usually ended up having to carry out treatment after Professor Ransome had done the diagnosis for most of his cases. Professor Ransome tried strongly to persuade him to specialise in Neurological Medicine but he chose to remain in General Medicine.

Those years at the Singapore General Hospital were busy years for him. He would often spend the night at his Upper Block laboratory — a small place out in the verandah. There was a bed there, in the midst of his equipment, slides and other paraphernalia, where he could sleep.

Watch by the sick,

enrich the poor

With blessings from

Thy boundless store;

Be every mourner's sleep

tonight,

Like infants;

slumbers, pure and light.

Sun of my soul,

Thou Saviour dear,

It is not night

if Thou be near;

O may no earthborn cloud

arise

To hide Thee

from Thy servant's eyes.

Sun Of My Soul

he day was
December the 8th,
1941. It was not quite morning.
In two to three hours' time the sun

would raise her bright face and flood the island
with her life-giving rays. Dr Chew, Hock Neo and their three
children were fast asleep in the verandah of their home at the
hospital grounds. Ten-year-old Chin Hin, his younger sister Ai
Lin, and little Jimmy took a longer time to fall asleep the
night before because they were excitedly anticipating the
following day's trip. All their bags were packed, and the
itinerary for their four-week holiday had been carefully
worked out by Dad. He would drive the family across to
Malacca and then go on to Cameron Highlands. But his plans
never materialised. In the midst of their slumber, events were
taking place that would drastically affect not only their lives
but the life of the whole region. Unknown to all, that same
night, the Japanese landed at Kota Bahru, the capital of
Kelantan, and had planned an air raid over Singapore.

It was about four o'clock in the morning when the Chew
family were rudely awakened by an ear-shattering explosion
which shook the house. The frantic wailing of the air-raid
sirens was heard soon after. Later, Dr Chew discovered that a

bomb had exploded just outside their home scattering shrapnel over a wide area. They could easily have been hit by the shrapnel if not for the protection offered by the verandah pillars of the house. But he knew that it was more than just walls that kept them safe.

News later got out that the Japanese had sent some seventeen naval bombers from their base in Southern Indo-China to Singapore. Most of their bombs were dropped on Tengah and Seletar airfields, the target of their attack, but some fell on the crowded section of town, causing about two hundred casualties. Within a few hours of the air raid, Dr Chew and other hospital staff had to attend to the steady stream of bomb casualties that were brought in. Many of them were Chettiars from the badly affected Chulia Street area. All leave was cancelled and it was to be many years later before the Chew family could enjoy a holiday.

In response to the attack, the British Eastern Fleet sent in their battleships, the HMS Repulse and the HMS Prince of Wales, the flag-ship. They set sail for the Malayan east coast toward the Japanese fleet. Two days later, they were fiercely attacked by several waves of enemy aircraft. Both ships were hit by aerial-torpedoes and sunk off the Kuantan coast, taking along with them a great number of men, and the confidence of the local people in the invincibility of the British.

The hospital staff got news of the incident in the next morning's papers. Some of them were terribly affected by the news; their morale ran low. The nursing sisters in particular wept in the duty room. Dr Chew was one of those who tried to comfort them, saying, "God is sovereign. He will see things through. He will see us through. It doesn't matter what happens."

It was this same confidence in a sovereign God that helped him overcome the disappointment of seeing one of the laboratories which he had started from scratch destroyed by a Japanese bomb that landed in the hospital area. Glassware, equipment, slides, specimens, and all else were smashed to bits. Glass splinters were strewn all over. His bed was wrecked and covered with debris. Most nights at that time, wearied after a hard day's labour, he would have been asleep on that very bed. Or else he would be bending over his microscope and studying his specimens. But that night, he was out on his rounds of the wards, taking specimens and attending to new cases. He was spared from death not by chance or sheer good luck but by the unseen and sovereign hand of God.

By January 1942, the hospitals began to be severely taxed with air-raid casualties and the wounded from the fighting forces. Hotels, schools and clubs had to be converted into emergency hospitals and first-aid depots to cope with the demand. The Singapore medical staff was augmented by medical officers, sisters, nurses, dressers who fled from upcountry Malaya as the Japanese forces advanced down the peninsula. In the General Hospital alone about eight thousand persons, patients, staff and refugees, were fed daily at the hospital canteen. Everyone worked under high pressure.

The medical officers could not deal with the dreadful rush of severely wounded casualties. All they could do sometimes was to give injections of morphine to ease the pain of the war-victims, as they were laid out on their stretchers in the corridors.

Reporting on the conditions at the hospitals, the Acting Chief Medical Officer, Dr Scrimgeour, wrote: "When the Japanese forces reached Johore Bahru, they began to shell Singapore and in February air-raids continued day and night. The continual bombing and shelling increased the stream of wounded pouring into aid-posts, depots and hospitals, and soon the hospitals were literally crammed with wounded civilian and military. The General Hospital, with normal accommodation for 830 patients, found itself at the end of the fighting with some 3 500, of whom 1 100 were service casualties and 2 400 civilian casualties.

"The Japanese forces landed on the island from the mainland on the morning of the 9th February; and from then onwards, as their pincers closed on the town, the work of the hospitals and aid-posts became progressively more difficult. The shelling and bombing and general turmoil of war taxed the morale of the staff to its utmost, and it can be safely stated that the personnel of the Medical Services came through this strange and terrifying ordeal with remarkable courage, calmness and devotion to duty."[5]

By mid-February all reservoirs were in Japanese hands. Most areas of town, including hospitals, had no water and the effect of this was paralysing. Without labour to clear the debris, bury the dead, or mend broken sewers, the town was filled with the stench of filth and death. The mortuary at the General Hospital was filled to the ceiling with dead bodies. It was this sight in particular that led the Chew's eldest boy, Chin Hin, to decide that he would become a doctor like his father.

In the face of such fierce onslaught from the enemy, General Arthur Percival, the Commander of the British Army in Malaya, surrendered. The document of surrender was signed in the Ford factory at Bukit Timah on 15 February 1942, the first day of the Lunar New Year. Then began a period of three-and-a-half years of occupation under the Japanese, one of the darkest periods in the lives of the people of Singapore. In the face of the uncertainties ahead, Dr Chew could be sure of only one thing — the faithfulness of One who promised never to leave him or forsake him.

5 Annual Report of the Medical Department, Colony of Singapore, 1946, p 4.

Other refuge

have I none,

Hangs my helpless soul

on Thee:

Leave, ah, leave me

not alone,

Still support

and comfort me.

All my trust

on Thee is stayed,

All my help

from Thee I bring;

Cover my defenceless

head

With the shadow

of Thy wing.

Jesus, Lover Of My Soul

The long convoy of ambulances, lorries and other vehicles snaked silently from Outram Road all the way to Yio Chu Kang Mental Hospital, passing along its way the ravages of war — ruined buildings, fallen lamp-posts and telephone poles, inextricable meshes of telephone wires, scarred landmarks. They formed a grim landscape.

Dr Chew and his family were huddled together in one of the lorries. Ai Lin had fallen asleep in his arms. Chin Hin had crept up close to him and was looking out into the sky, his innocent mind brooding over the gruesome facts of war — thoughts too heavy for a child to bear, seed-thoughts that would bear fruit in his future endeavours. Jimmy, too young to be seriously preoccupied over the current happenings, was fast asleep by his mother's side. Hock Neo had one arm wrapped around him and the other lay gently on the child that was yet to be. With her head resting on the bundles of their hurriedly packed belongings, she soon fell asleep. Dr Chew's gaze fell on each one of his family and he was suddenly overwhelmed by a sense of complete helplessness. All that he could do in the face of their uncertain future was to entrust them into God's care and protection; in short, to trust God completely.

That morning, the Chew family, together with 800 civilian patients, other medical officers and their families, sisters, nurses, and other hospital staff, were ordered to leave the General Hospital and to move to Miyako Byoin, the new name the Japanese gave to the Mental Hospital. They were told not to bring any medical equipment and supplies, but undaunted by the orders, the sisters and nurses secretly brought with them knives, forceps, medicines and whatever else they could hide amongst the "kapok" in the pillows that they took along. It turned out to be a very wise move as they had very little to work with at the Mental Hospital.

As the lorries rolled on, the previous day's unhappy events flashed across Dr Chew's mind. The fierce-looking frontline troops took over the hospital and went on a senseless and destructive rampage. Anger and resentment welled up afresh in his heart as he saw again in his mind's eye how the X-ray plants, electro-cardiogram and other laboratory equipment were smashed up. His precious findings on some 2 600 ECGs that he had painstakingly recorded over the years were either burnt or thrown in the drain. They were part of his preparation for the further specialist examinations which he had planned to take in London after the family holiday. But the war crushed his hopes for further education. He was further horrified as he recalled the brutal massacre at Alexandra Hospital, and the shelling of Kandang Kerbau Maternity Hospital where Dr Norris and Dr Sinha , who were his personal friends and a midwife were killed by stray shrapnel. Still fresh in his mind was the awful sight of the innocent civilian bomb casualties that filled the hospital wards. Other incidences of Japanese atrocities related to him by eye-witnesses came to mind. He hated these cruel men.

They finally reached their destination and were met by fully-armed sentry guards who started to yell at them in Japanese. Dr Chew began to imagine the worst. He thought they would suffer a similar fate to that of the numerous other victims of Japanese brutality. Fearful though they were, another senior doctor and he scrambled out of their lorries to find out what the guards wanted. The men shouted and gesticulated wildly and Dr Chew was finally able to interpret their communication to mean, "Have the children had any food?" Relieved but bewildered by their uncharacteristic compassion, he shook his head vigorously. At that instant he felt the Lord's rebuke for having hated these men so completely. His heart softened toward them and he willingly acknowledged their redeeming feature — their love for children. Nonetheless he found it difficult to reconcile their tenderheartedness toward children with their heartless and vicious brutality toward adult men and women. He stood there amazed as they brought out crate after crate

of milk for the children. This helped save the lives of not only
the children but quite a number of patients too. And it taught
him never to hate another human and to seek to discover the
good in another.

Then followed the task of transferring the patients from the
vehicles to the hospital bunks. They had only bare wooden
bunks for beds. Some of them were put on mattresses
brought over from the General Hospital. They did whatever
they could to accommodate all the patients. There was a
Japanese Director but he was not in control. They had the
military with them. The doctors and other hospital workers
were made to wear identification armbands and badges.

At Miyako the Chews had to share their living quarters
with four other families and one bachelor. They had to
divide the space amongst themselves. Hock Neo was
soon busying herself with setting up home in one
corner of the dining room, and the other housewives did
likewise with their own corners. Though initially everyone was
saddened by the recent unfortunate events, that soon gave
way to a spirit of co-operation. They functioned as one family
and the fellowship they experienced helped to buoy up their
spirits through that trying period of their lives.

They had the European personnel with them until they were
interned in early March. About 3 000 internees were confined
to the Changi Prison which was built to house only 600
prisoners. The 106 doctors who were interned served at the

Prison Hospital. However, one medical officer, one surgeon and one eye specialist were permitted to remain at Miyako. Together with the local doctors, they pulled together all the skills they had between them and made a job of it. Their motto was, "Be Prepared." This positive mental attitude together with their spirit of cooperation and their ingenuity enabled them to make the most of their limited resources. Whatever they lacked in terms of equipment and apparatus, they cleverly improvised. Dr Chew had a hand in making his own apparatus. He was very much involved in treating patients suffering from tuberculosis. They did not have any medicines, so he resorted mostly to collapsing tubercular lungs by putting in air, a method called artificial pneumothorax. Another method called pneumoperitoneum was to put air into the abdominal cavity to collapse the lung from below. He had to make his own apparatus to perform these operations which involved bending glass tubes over a flame and fixing them to glass bottles. His homemade apparatus served him right through the Occupation.

At Miyako, Ben's day began at about seven in the morning and work would be done by about six in the evening and the rest of the day was spent with his family. The already crowded household was to receive a new member that October. Ernest, the Chew's fifth and last child was born on 18 October 1942 after a four-week wait at St Andrew's Mission Hospital. Friends, Dr and Mrs Ho Boon Liat, who were in charge at the hospital had looked after Hock Neo and handled the delivery. Those were busy days for Ben. He would commute between Miyako and St Andrew's every evening by bus to be with his wife.

Ernest was born wrinkled and wizened, totally unlike other babies. Two months later, he was far from being in the pink of health; pink he most certainly was, but healthy he was not. His hands and feet were bright pink and icy cold, and he was struggling about obviously in pain and much discomfort. Ben got Dr Haridas, the child specialist from Kandang Kerbau Hospital, to look him over and he remarked, "I've never seen anything like this before."

"What about Pink Disease?" Ben suggested. He recalled reading about this particular nutritional disease which occurred in Scandinavia.

"Oh," Haridas replied, "It's possible although it doesn't quite fit in as Pink Disease. But I'll tell you what. We'll give him all the vitamins we can." Fortunately, vitamins were in good supply. Ernest did get better and he developed into quite a healthy baby. Many children and adults suffered from malnutrition, especially beri-beri; and the vitamin B that the Japanese supplied saved many lives.

Apart from malnutrition, the hospital received patients suffering from malaria, pneumonia and with a large majority of tuberculosis and dysentery cases. The patients were generally a grateful lot. The doctors and their families owed their existence to their patients. Their pay of about 250 Japanese dollars a month, as the days went on, could not bring in much food. In the latter part of the Occupation, one egg would cost the ludicrous sum of about $200! They managed to survive mostly on the generosity and kindness of patients who brought in sacks of rice, bananas, meat, eggs and other foodstuffs. Sometimes Dr Chew and his family would have a dish of bean sprouts which Hock Neo grew herself. She also grew tapioca from which she would make tapioca bread. Their friends from outside also brought in food for them.

It was heartwarming to have patients who could empathise with their doctor's difficulties and limitations. Once Dr Chew treated a very young man who had a tubercular joint. Ben and the other doctors told him honestly, "We have nothing. We can only put you at rest, tie you up and put you in plaster." There was no word of complaint from him at all. He understood the situation perfectly and said, "Sure, sure, quite alright." After about six months they removed the cast, started him on exercises and he was completely cured. What was unforgettable was his cheerfulness throughout his stay. The cooperation between staff and patients and the excellent working relationships between the Colonial Medical Officers and the local officers helped to encourage Ben during those trying circumstances at Miyako.

What further encouraged him was to see other people carry on with their lives almost unaffected by the war — the farmers next door for one. They would be up before the sun, gather their vegetables and leave for the market to make their sale. Life went on uninterrupted. They faithfully went about their daily business. There was also a leper camp next to where Ben lived, and he would see the leper patients bending over their handicraft, patiently working on their items. These scenes reminded Ben that life had to be lived a day at a time, faithfully putting one's hands to each day's tasks to the best of one's ability, resting in God's providence and trusting in His lovingkindness.

19

In death's dark vale

I fear no ill

With Thee, dear Lord,

beside me;

Thy rod and staff

my comfort still,

Thy cross before

to guide me.

The King of love

my Shepherd is,

Whose goodness

faileth never;

I nothing lack

if I am His,

And He is mine

forever.

**The King Of Love
My Shepherd Is**

he Japanese
officer in charge of
the Civilian Medical Service,
Dr Kozo Ando, was one who
sincerely desired to help the local population
and medical staff. It was through his instigation and advice
that on 23 November 1942 the whole hospital staff left
Miyako Byoin for Tan Tock Seng Hospital(TTSH). Its proximity
to town meant that more people could avail themselves of
the services, and for the medical staff this move meant better
facilities and living conditions. Tan Tock Seng Hospital,
renamed Hakuai Byoin by the Japanese, became the main
civil hospital. The medical staff was increased by the
recruitment of a few more doctors and comprised surgeons,
an anaesthetist, ophthalmologists, dentists, medical doctors,
pathologists, a matron, senior nurses, a pharmacist,
laboratory staff and other general staff. Dr W A Balhetchet
was appointed the Chief Medical Officer to direct the medical
work. He was an excellent administrator; he organised the
staff into groups and Dr Chew was made head of one of the
medical units.

To the Chew family, their new accommodation at Hakuai —
a three-bedroom two-storey terrace house — was like a

mansion. It took a while to get used to all that space. It had a verandah and a backyard. Typical of their generous spirit, it was not long before they took in "refugees" — Hock Neo's sister and brother-in-law and Ben's brother. They settled in quite comfortably. He and Hock Neo soon had vegetables and tapioca growing in their backyard, a few hens running around and two pigs, gifts from patients. The pigs became household pets; one of them was affectionately named Carlo by the children. The pigs were washed and scrubbed clean and had ribbons tied around their necks. Little Ernest in particular grew very fond of them and was grieved when they finally had to be slaughtered for food. He refused to eat the meat and has never liked pork since then.

Again, as in Miyako, the patients would give food to the staff in appreciation of their service. Another source of supply was from the doctor's periodic trips to Bahau, a Eurasian farming settlement in Malaya set up by the Japanese. Dr Balhatchet had arranged these trips to obtain medical supplies. Equipment, expendable materials and drugs became more and more scarce as the Occupation period dragged out, but the medical staff did their best to eke out the available medical stocks through those three-and-a-half years. They relied first on good nursing, and used medicines only as a last resort.

They worked longer hours at Hakuai; the staff were working night and day. Ben had less time for the family; he would be back for lunch and dinner, then hurry back to work till about ten in the evening and after an hour's break he would be back at the wards, returning home to sleep before starting work again at about seven the next morning. When on call he would be up all the time. Patients would come in at any time, even in the middle of the night. Many of the staff were Christians but they did not go to church on Sundays because they had so much work to do and also to stay clear of the Kempeitai. But they did meet for informal times of prayer and Bible reading. These were not organised meetings but happened rather spontaneously between two or more Christian doctors. One of their main petitions to God was for a speedy end to the war. The nurses worked on an eight-hour shift round the clock. Younger male members of the staff were also given guard duties by the Japanese for the security of the hospital. Each group of three or four staff was required to patrol the grounds for a two to three-hour session from seven in the evening to seven in the morning.

Dr Chew was in charge of the tuberculosis work because of his experience and had two doctors and a nurse assisting him. Between them they handled more than 2 000 cases. The treatment was laborious because there were no drugs such as streptomycin. For unilateral cases, air had to be measured and pushed into the pleural cavity of the lungs using a homemade apparatus. Then they had to check the success of the operation by X-raying the lungs. Complications such as "pleural effusion" would sometimes arise which required their further attention.

The general cases were a pitiful lot. A lot of patients suffered from dysentery, malnutrition, various fevers and pneumonia. The mortality rate was quite high because of poor nourishment and the lack of medication. Dr Chew was hardest hit when his own mother became a victim of dysentery towards the end of the Occupation. He was hopeful when her condition initially improved, but later it took a sudden turn for the worse and she died of a haemorrhage to the deep sorrow of the family.

One particular positive experience for Dr Chew was the wonderful way that his colleague's life was saved. Dr C E Smith had developed a lung abscess which threatened his life. Dr Chew who was looking after him managed to get hold of some injections of sulphonamides but they did not help and his condition became critical and there was nothing further he could do to help him. At that time they received information from the underground that the American Air Force had dropped some medical supplies over the Sime Road Prison Camp for internees. The hospital pathologist, Dr L S da Silva, risked a trip to the camp and returned with some injections of the wonder drug "penicillin" which was unheard of in Singapore. Dr Chew then started treatment on Dr Smith and became the first person to use penicillin in Singapore. Dr Smith's condition improved under his care and the excellent

nursing the hospital nurses provided. He was then sent to
London for a completely successful surgery.

Things did not work out so fortunately for two of the
European doctors from the prisoner of war camp who
were tortured and placed in cells by the Kempeitai, the
Japanese secret police. Dr Bowyer eventually
developed dysentery and passed away. Dr Stanley when
brought in for further interrogation tried to escape torture by
jumping out of a window and died as a result. In memory of
them and Dr Norris who died earlier during the War, the three
blocks at the Singapore General Hospital were renamed
Bowyer Block, Stanley Block and Norris Block.

The threat of being caught and tortured by the Kempeitai
did not deter Dr Chew and his colleagues from secretly
supplying medicine and money to the internees. The secret
transaction took place quite regularly in the X-ray department.
A sick internee was sometimes sent to Hakuai for treatment.
They would invariably decide that he should have an X-ray
even though he may have had only a stomach-ache or the flu.
The guard would accompany the patient into the X-ray room
but he would not be able to see a thing. The doctors could
see him clearly because they had been in the room for some
time and had got used to the darkness. Taking advantage of
this situation, they would slip the medicines or money into
the patient's pocket, after which the patient would leave
escorted by the unsuspecting guard. This practice stopped

after the "Double Tenth" incident. On 10 October 1943, a few ships in the harbour had been blown up by mines. This incident sparked off a purge amongst civilians and prisoners of war. It served to add fuel to Dr Chew's dislike for the Japanese. Another incident at the hospital increased further his prejudice against them.

There was a Japanese matron at Hakuai and there was also a Japanese doctor, a medical graduate from Berlin. One day, Dr Chew saw them talking by the grass verge along the path leading to the operating theatre. Suddenly he slapped her, causing her to fall to the ground. She got up almost immediately, bowed to him and walked off. Dr Chew stood there horrified. Straightaway he reported the matter to Dr Balhatchet: "Bally, you've got to report this to the Japanese Director. We cannot allow such disrespect to the person and office of Matron. He may do the same to our local nurses; that would be bad for their morale and I don't think they would want to work with us anymore." The matter was promptly dealt with and the Matron was profuse in her thanks to them.

mongst his patients were about fifty Japanese soldiers suffering from tuberculosis. They occupied a whole ward and Dr Chew was treating them. Although he disliked the Japanese, it did not prevent him from doing his best for them. One day, on his regular rounds, he came across a new patient. He noticed a Bible on his locker.

Curious, he queried, "Are you a Christian?"

"Yes, I'm a member of the Methodist Church in Tokyo," he replied. He showed Dr Chew his family portrait, his wife and three children aged between three and nine years. "I know I'll never see them again," he said in a plaintive voice. Dr Chew then prayed together with him. During the time that he was there, they had several good times praying, reading the Bible and talking together; Dr Chew in his broken Japanese. Through their friendship, he sensed the Lord's gentle rebuke for having hated the Japanese. He acknowledged and confessed his lack of love and his hidden resentment toward them and asked for grace to love his enemies, which is the Christian response. From then on his service was charged with a new spirit — that of love and not of mere duty. This was one of the deepest lessons he learnt during the Occupation. Years later, in early 1989, at a meeting of the Evangelical Fellowship Of Singapore (EFOS), when Joseph Tsutada, the President of Evangelical Fellowship of Asia, asked the meeting for forgiveness for all the atrocities of the Japanese War, as Chairman of EFOS, Dr Chew's reply was, "We also seek your forgiveness for having hated the Japanese." Joseph was astonished and deeply touched by his response. God's Spirit had brought about this new mind and heart toward his enemies during the Occupation and this same spirit would characterise Ben's attitude toward his fellow men. He would always seek the good in another.

As the atomic mushroom clouds rose ominously above the towns of Hiroshima and Nagasaki in August 1945, the world waited for the final surrender of Japan. For Singapore the day came on 12 September 1945. The end of the Occupation in Singapore was declared with the lowering of the rising-sun flag of Japan at the Town Hall, and in its place was raised the Union Jack signifying the beginning of the period of the British Military Administration (BMA) under whom the country gradually came to live again.

20

I don't know

about tomorrow,

It may bring me

poverty,

But the one

who feeds the sparrow,

Is the one

who stands by me.

And the path

that be my portion,

May be through

the flame or flood,

But His presence

goes before me,

And I'm covered

with His blood.

I Don't Know About Tomorrow

he three-and-a-half years of Japanese Occupation gave the local personnel opportunities to exercise their initiative. With the internment of European personnel, they had to assume full responsibility for the medical services and they passed the test with flying colours. The doctors, nurses, dentists, dressers and general staff showed that, despite having been excluded from the higher echelons of the medical service, they were able, by maximising their abilities and by sheer hard work and determination, to run the hospital services as efficiently as possible under those trying and difficult conditions.

This new-found confidence encouraged the local officers to request that the Colonial authorities do away with the two-tier service, the Colonial Medical Service and the Local Medical Service. Dr Chew was voted the scribe at the meeting. On behalf of his colleagues, he penned a long letter to the Secretary of State for the Colonies describing how well they worked together as one medical service and advocating that Colonial and Local officers work as equals in the profession. Within a month the reply came from London endorsing all that they had written and affirming that that would be the best direction to take, bearing in mind the challenges ahead for the Medical Service in the aftermath of the war. It was only three years later that the unification of the two Medical Services came into being — a good that arose out of the difficult years of Japanese Occupation. As a result of the unification, more medical personnel were sent overseas for specialist training and returned to hold senior positions. By then Dr Chew had already left the government service and was practising medicine from his father-in-law's pharmacy.

His resignation took place not too long after the Japanese surrender. The British Military Administration took over the medical department. They found themselves with a population that was very much undernourished and riddled with tuberculosis, beri-beri, malaria, dysentery, and other diseases. All hospitals and available clinics were briskly organised on an emergency basis to reach as many of the neglected population as possible. The General Hospital at Outram Road which was occupied by the military was turned into a Civilian General Hospital. Dr Chew was appointed to run the Medical Unit there and to concentrate their efforts on treating only acute medical cases. He welcomed the appointment, but uppermost on his mind were the 2 400 TB patients who were receiving treatment at Tan Tock Seng Hospital. The hard facts of the TB scourge were difficult for him to ignore.

"Fine," he responded, "thank you for putting me in charge;

but what about the TB cases?"

The Chief Administrator, Colonel Walkingshaw, a surgeon at General Hospital since pre-war days, officiously replied, "Don't worry about that. You know, we've got to do first things first. You just take orders." TB was obviously not a priority in their medical scheme at the time.

Dr Chew proposed a compromise. He would do both jobs — serve at the GH and in the afternoons or evenings attend to his TB patients at TTSH. "Allow me to do that so we can keep the patients," he appealed. "I can't leave the TB cases." The reply he received was most disquieting.

"No. The government has made its policy," came the uncompromising reply from the Colonel. "Your cases, Chew, can go to the streets."

Crossed, he returned home to discuss the matter with his wife. "This is against medical ethics," he concluded after narrating the whole incident.

"Christian ethics," Hock Neo added. They brought the matter to the Lord in prayer and agreed that he should leave government service.

So he resigned from the government service. It was a costly decision. It meant forgoing a $27 000 pension, the widow's and orphan's fund, the opportunity for further studies and promotion to the higher medical service. But what was more important to him was to remain true to himself and his Christian convictions; he served the Divine Master. He and

Hock Neo had the opportunity to apply the verse they had chosen to be their life verse: "...seek ye first the kingdom of God, and His righteousness; and all these things shall be added unto you (Matthew 6:33)." The verse prior to this one in the Bible reads, "So don't worry and don't keep saying, 'What shall we eat, what shall we drink or what shall we wear?' That is what pagans are always looking for; your Heavenly Father knows that you need them all."

Dr Chew and his family would have to leave the spacious accommodation at Tan Tock Seng Hospital and squeeze into one of the rooms at his father-in-law's Geylang house. Dr Chew could practise from his pharmacy. It was really a step of faith because they had no money; they could not even pay their insurance premiums. Putting his trust in the faithfulness of his Heavenly Father, he remained steadfast about his decision. And "all these things" did come to him as a matter of course. One of his patients offered him a three-room semi-detached house in Branksome Road at a very low rental. He saw this as the Lord's confirmation of his decision. He felt it was God who provided them with that home. He was kept very busy at his private practice as he was treating about a hundred tuberculosis cases a day.

His chief concern was not for his personal situation but for the many tuberculosis sufferers. For every patient that came to him, there were many others suffering in oblivion. The disease thrived, especially in the numerous dark, ill-ventilated and overcrowded cubicles at Chinatown. His former colleague, Dr B R Sreenivasan, was keeping up the fight at Kandang Kerbau Hospital, but he eventually resigned when he was unjustifiably denied further training which was due to him.

Something had to be done; Dr Chew did not wait long to take action on the matter. He spoke to some friends from the business world and some of his doctor friends also presented the sombre facts and challenged them to help to finance the effort to combat TB. The result was the formation of the Singapore Anti-Tuberculosis Association, SATA , led by company director Mr S H Peek. The work was launched with much prayer. Those among the group who were Christians prayed very hard for the welfare of the local population. Dr Chew was asked to be in charge of the work , but he had to turn down the offer as he had far too many of his own TB cases to handle, his private practice to run and responsibilities at church. He was satisfied to have played a part in founding SATA. The Association was registered on 23 August 1947. The singleminded effort and steady zeal of the people behind SATA developed it into an institution which succeeded in bringing TB under better control. The BMA failed to give priority to the pressing problem of TB; but God had raised help from another quarter because Dr Chew and his friends had cried out to Him for help and acted in faith. Less than a

year later the Rotary Tuberculosis Clinic founded by the
Government and the Rotary Club was opened at the TTSH;
and after two years it was converted into a TB hospital. Finally
the government was "persuaded" to take on the TB problem.
TB eventually became so well-controlled that TTSH later
became again a general hospital. With the situation under
control, Dr Chew was handling more normal medical cases at
his clinic.

He was receiving many patients — young and old, rich and
poor and his practice was doing so well that he was
eventually able to buy a large piece of property at St Patrick's
Road, right next to the sea, on which he built a beautiful
bungalow by the sea for his family. He named it "Charis," the
Greek word for "grace." He never dreamt of owning such a
beautiful place, certainly never planned to. He lived by the
"day-by-day" principle; "don't worry at all then about
tomorrow. Tomorrow can take care of itself! One day's
trouble is enough for one day"— that was the advice Jesus
gave and that was how he lived.

The sale of the property and the shift in 1978 to 50
Kingsmead Road followed family consultation and prayer and
a unanimous agreement. All those living on the property had
homes of their own and only a few still stayed at the main
house. There was no more sea! High rise buildings and busy
roads had taken its place. After much searching, the new
house at Kingsmead Road was found to be ideal. Jim and

Selene, on a visit to Keswick, brought back a Keswick-stone plate. It was inscribed "CHARIS."

All to Jesus

I surrender,

All to Him

I freely give;

I will ever

love and trust Him,

In His service

daily live.

I surrender all,

I surrender all,

All to Thee,

my blessed Saviour,

I surrender all.

I Surrender All

**r Chew's** attitude toward his possessions has always been that of a steward. The large piece of land he owned was also enjoyed by other people. Friends and church brethren in need of accommodation lived in the adjoining houses. About half a dozen families and singles benefitted in this way. He invited his youngest sister, Anne and her husband to build their house on his land. His father and another sister Ada and her family lived in one of the houses for a period of time. On Saturday afternoons, the field in the middle of his property was filled with the happy voices of young people at play. These were the Crusaders, the Young People's Group (YPG) from Bethesda Katong where he is an elder. Many young people from other churches were baptised in the sea opposite.

When Dr Chew was sixteen years old, he was one of the young leaders in the Young People's Group in Bethesda Bras Basah Road. It was Mr Tipson, an elder of the Church and director of the British and Foreign Society who encouraged him to preach.

"You've got to be a speaker," he said.

"Me? A speaker?" Ben asked incredulously. "No, I'll never

be a speaker. I'll be a personal worker." But Mr Tipson would not take no for an answer and insisted that he spoke the following week at the YPG meeting. He did not want Ben to refer to his notes.

"You should more or less know what's in your notes...speak!"

So at the following YPG meeting, the first year medical student nervously delivered his first message without notes to about 20 young people. Mr Tipson sat with some older men at the back, listening intently to his every word. He spoke for about twenty minutes, but it seemed like hours. Later in a personal session Mr Tipson remarked, "You packed enough material for ten sermons!" The reluctant preacher-to-be spoke three more times until Mr Tipson felt he could be on his own. Three years later, as a deacon of the church, Dr Chew was invited to speak at church services. Having grown up in Bethesda Bras Basah Road, he had the opportunity to sit at the feet of gifted expositors like Messrs E Tipson, A J Turner and Sydney Dant. Visiting speakers like Dr Donald Grey Barnhouse, Mr J O Sanders and others also helped to stir up a deep and lasting zeal in him to teach and preach the Word of God faithfully.

He was also the church organist and secretary and had to record the minutes for the elder's meetings. He taught at the Sunday School, helped with the youth work, played the organ, and took on speaking engagements — all these over and above his heavy load at General Hospital. Though he saw his main mission as a Christian doctor, he never let out of his mind church associations and church work. Involvement with the church was as natural as breathing for him.

In 1931, the elders of the Bras Basah Road Assembly decided that outreach work should be started in the Katong area. A Sunday School was first started at a rented shophouse at East Coast Road. The elders of the church and Miss Gladys Grigg, a missionary, tirelessly visited homes along the dusty Eng Kiam Place, Ceylon Road, Carpmael Road and other side roads to invite children to their Sunday School. Within a year about 50 children and teenagers filled the church hall. Gospel services in Malay and Chinese were later started. An adjoining shop house was rented. It soon became evident to the elders that a property was needed for the growing work. They brought their request before God.

Unknown to the elders, God was already working in the heart of Mr Wee Thiam Seng, a retired banker and a new Christian and member of the Brethren Assembly. He was walking by the auctioneers at Chulia Street one morning in 1934 and decided to go in. That day an 8 000 square feet piece of land at the junction of Carpmael Road and Pennefather Road was being auctioned. He made a bid which was unchallenged and the property became his for $1 700. The next day, being aware of the elder's prayers, he offered it for the Lord's work. God had wonderfully provided.

The brethren from the Bras Basah Assembly living in Katong were urged to attend the new church and so Dr Chew became associated with Bethesda Katong.

After Singapore's liberation from the Japanese Occupation, the door of the extended church was formally opened by Mrs B Chew at the Dedication Service on 15 September 1947. On 30 April 1948 Dr Chew was appointed an overseer of the Bethesda Katong Church and had as fellow elders, Mr Ong Tiang Tye, Dr Khoo Peng Seng, Mr T W G Knowles, and Mr A J Turner. Together with several others who joined the eldership later (Mr T C Koh in 1952) , they were led to start off several other outreaches for the Brethren Church.

Dr Chew learnt to have a wider vision for evangelism through the example of leaders such as Mr Tommy Knowles. A consulting engineer with Richie and Bisset, the foremost engineering company in Singapore, Mr T W G Knowles took over the leadership of the YPG from Mr Tipson. He would regularly lead several of the young people including Dr Chew to go tracting as far as Batu Pahat in Johore. The party would consist of two to three carloads of young people and they would distribute tracts to Malay fishermen and village folk some of whom received them gratefully .

hus Dr Chew learnt in his youth the importance of reaching out to the unreached beyond Singapore. His interest in missions led him to eventually be the China Inland Mission's (CIM; later renamed Overseas Missionary

Fellowship, OMF) choice as one of their Directors and also
Chairman of the Singapore Home Council, a position he held
until April 1987 when he made way for the new full-time
Home Director, Mr Kenneth Tan. He remains a Consulting
Director for OMF International. Prior to the formation of the
Home Council, CIM was closed to Asians. Dr Chew's vision
was for all local churches to be involved in overseas
outreach.

Dr Chew faithfully served the public as a private doctor, led
his brethren as an elder of the church, taught God's Word in
Sunday classes, preached at meetings, and supported parachurch work until his fifties when he arrived at the second
critical point in his life. The decision he made as a thirteen-
year old in his school chapel which determined his eternal
destiny was the first critical point in his life. This time it
wasn't the school chapel but the church hall. It wasn't a
schoolmate who was sitting next to him, it was his dear wife.
The speaker was his esteemed friend — Mr J O Sanders. He
wasn't preaching from Psalm 1; he spoke on discipleship. In
his straightforward, simple and clear style, he taught that
unless a Christian denied himself and died to his own desires
he was not totally committed to Christ. Such a Christian, the
Lord could not use for His glory.

Immediately, Dr Chew thought of his recent aspirations to
go into politics. He had been invited to join the political arena
and he was thinking about what he could do for the welfare

of the nation from this position of influence. He had brought the matter before the Lord and was taken up with the idea of bringing glory to God through what he could do as a political leader.

As he sat there listening, the Lord showed him the subtle difference between accomplishing something for Him and letting Him accomplish something through one's self. He had not come to the point of total surrender to the will of God in his life. His thoughts were interrupted by Mr Sander's solemn appeal at the end of his sermon: "I advise anyone who feels the Lord is asking him to be a disciple, and saying that he must deny himself and die to self, to please stand up."

Dr Chew stood up immediately. His wife knew what he was thinking about. That act of commitment must have meant different things to the various ones who stood up. But for Dr Chew it was a decision to go on to do the Lord's work in the Lord's way and according to His timing. God showed him that the way of true discipleship was death to self, and allowing Him to work through him in His way to accomplish great things for His glory and His alone. In obedient submission he was now free for the real purpose God had for him in the spiritual arena — to engage in the battle for the souls of his fellowmen — a cause for which he fought wholeheartedly, faithfully and, for most of the time, quietly.

So down the years he became personally involved with

many young people in the outreach of his church, but also workers and leaders in many parachurch bodies in their work as the arms and instruments of Singapore churches. He was to become God's instrument to rally Singapore Christians in a massive evangelistic effort in December 1978 with Billy Graham as the evangelist. Dr Chew was unanimously elected by church leaders as Chairman of the Billy Graham Evangelical Crusade. His leadership marshalled the overwhelming support the Crusade enjoyed — 237 out of the 265 Protestant congregations committed themselves to the Crusade. God had prepared the Church for this hour, and him for the Chairmanship. His wide acceptance by the English-speaking and Chinese-speaking churches and para-church organisations had made possible the unity that was so crucial for the success of the Crusade. Both Jim and Ernest also served on the Executive Committee. The week long Crusade was held at the 50 000-capacity National Stadium. It was the first time the Stadium was used by the private sector. It was filled to capacity and passed the 70 000 mark on the last night. Never was there a united witness of such magnitude. Even President Benjamin Sheares, Dr Chew's childhood friend, gave his support. When Dr Chew brought Dr Graham to see him, he remarked, "Dr Graham, God is going to bless the Crusade and I have been praying for it twice daily for a year!" Dr Chew noted that his friend must have continued the habit since their Sunday School days, advocated by their

Sunday School teacher, of having two devotional sessions daily.

His humble submission to God's will for his life had set the course of his life such that it availed him as God's special instrument during this critical point of Singapore's evangelical history.

21

TANJONG KATON, SINGAPORE.

The youth of the world

for the Man of Galilee!

The youth of the world

from all sin and self set free!

Ev'ry talent

pledg'd in service

Now and through

eternity,

The youth of the world

for the Man of Galilee!

The Youth Of The World

he mid-fifties was a time of marked juvenile delinquency particularly in the Katong area. Dr Chew and fellow elders of Bethesda Katong were increasingly concerned for the youth who were involved in secret societies and gangsterism. They were hit closer home when a youth whom they recognised as having been to their Sunday School was sentenced to life imprisonment for his involvement in a murder. His gang members received the death sentence, but he was spared as he was underaged. Church-based activities and the open-air meetings which they attempted had failed to attract these young people. As a result of youth work and the Prison Ministry, in which Dr Chew shared for many years, hundreds have been won for Christ. This young man, in particular, was remarkably converted. He is now a well-known and beloved pastor and an outstanding evangelist.

At the same time the population structure in Singapore had changed drastically from the adult, male dominated society of the 1900's. "Youths dominated the scene in the 1950's. To provide education for the emerging generation, the government had embarked on large-scale programmes to train thousands of teachers and build scores of new schools... Christian missions could not keep up with the government in its educational efforts... The relative influence of the church on the student population must, therefore, decline with time".[6]

These sets of circumstances weighed on Dr Chew's heart very much. Feeling very much their helplessness in the face of the desperate situation, the elders of Bethesda Katong turned to God for help. They prayed regularly for the youth problem not knowing how God would answer their prayers. But God was actively at work and was raising up help from an unexpected quarter, thousands of miles away from where they were.

Veteran Youth For Christ worker, Rev Joe Weatherly had returned to the United States after organising Youth For Christ in India. Youth For Christ International had requested him to go to Australia and New Zealand, but no support was forthcoming. He was frustrated.

One evening, after a missionary meeting at Toccoa Falls College in North Georgia, Joe half-jokingly said to the Head of the college's Music Department, "John, why don't you and I go to Singapore? You'll be the King and I'll be the Prime Minister." No sooner had the sound of their laughter receded when Joe felt the Lord's gentle rebuke. He excused himself, went into a room and addressed his Master, "Lord, I said something wrong. What was it?" In his inner being he heard

6 Sng, Bobby, p 245.

his Lord reply, "I've been trying to talk to you about Singapore for a long time, but you wouldn't listen."

With a will trained in obedience, Joe wasted no time in contacting Bob Cook, President of Youth For Christ International, and presented the idea to him. It was green light all the way. Bob approved the idea and in less than ten days all the necessary support was pledged where for nearly a year nothing had come in for Australia and New Zealand.

Joe and his wife Bernice knew then that the Lord wanted them in Singapore. With the Lord's assurance and His word to Joe in John 4:38 that He was sending him to "reap that wherein he had bestowed no labour," the Weatherlys left the States for Singapore. It was in September 1956 that Joe and Bernice Weatherly arrived in Singapore. The timing of their arrival was perfect. The situation was ripe. The church was wanting and waiting.

That same evening Mr Gordon Scott, an elder of Bethesda Katong, was at the airport to see a friend off. Whilst waiting, he noticed Joe. Thinking that he "looked like a Christian," he approached him in order to get acquainted. When he learnt that Joe was from Youth For Christ and was in Singapore for the sole purpose of exploring youth evangelism, he lost no time in getting him to meet Dr Chew and the other elders.

After meeting him, the elders were convinced that Joe was God's answer to their prayers. Who but He could have masterminded the meeting of the two parties — a very experienced youth worker and a group of local Christians burdened for the thousands of youth searching for direction in life.

"Rev Weatherly saw the possibilities and immediately set about recruiting scores of voluntary workers mostly from Bethesda Katong Church. Together, they sparked off a campaign to reach Singapore's youth on a scale never before attempted".[7] This was the birth of Singapore Youth For Christ — God's answer to the earnest prayers of His concerned people.

Dr Chew and the elders of Bethesda Katong were very supportive of Joe's efforts right from the start. They took the lead in providing direction and support to Joe and his team of volunteers. The Saturday Night Rallies, training camps called Keen Teen Crusades and School Clubs attracted the young people. The first eight years of Singapore Youth For Christ's existence had resulted in 10 000 conversions!

One unforgettable experience for Dr Chew was when he became evangelist at one of the rallies due to a sudden change in plans. Joe Weatherly had without advance notice asked Dr Chew to replace him as evangelist for the evening rally. Although Dr Chew had tried to excuse himself saying, "I'm not a gospel preacher," Joe could not be made to change his mind.

The night rally was held at the badminton hall of Raffles

7 Sng, Bobby, p 246.

Institution. Dr Chew arrived early and stood on the second floor of the school building from where he could see scores of young people rushing up the staircase that led to the hall. He could sense their enthusiasm and excitement as they filled up the hall. From the size of the crowd it looked like it was going to be a "double-header," that is two rallies held one after another with a half hour break between them.

The programme moved briskly and the time came for Dr Chew to speak. As he stood before at least 200 young people that evening, he told them about the Lord Jesus Christ. He spoke about His death on the cross and how He rose victoriously from the dead. When he gave an invitation to those who wanted to receive Christ as their personal Saviour and Lord, he beheld a most wonderful sight — close to fifty young people stood up and responded in faith. The same thing happened in the second rally. This time about sixty more responded. Never had he seen so many people turning to Christ all at one time after a simple preaching of the gospel. And the same result was repeated rally after rally. It was indeed a time of reaping among Singapore's youth.

In 1959 Joe left Singapore, having handed over the reins in the capable hands of Singapore Youth For Christ's first Asian Director, Liew Kee Kok, an active member of Bethesda Katong whom he had earlier groomed for this role. A Board was formed with Dr Chew as its President, a position he has held to this day, from which he faithfully offers support, advice

and encouragement to Singapore Youth For Christ's various
Directors through the years.[8]

As young people were brought into a personal
relationship with Christ and into the church by the
hundreds, the Christian youth population grew. The
Christian influence had an obvious effect on the youth
problem.

Dr Chew could see how the church and the parachurch
body complemented one another in building the Kingdom of
God. He realised that the contribution of evangelistic and
mission ministries could be a tremendous impetus to church
growth and ministry in Singapore. He so caught the flame of
true discipleship and evangelistic fervour that he continues
always to free himself for the sake of the Gospel of Jesus
Christ and the cause of Christianity through his support of
numerous Christian organisations, and endeavours to share
this zeal with others as elder and teacher.

8 In July 1991, he handed the Chairmanship over to Mr Hia Chek Phang but he continues as President
  Emeritus.

22

For the joy

of human love,

Brother, sister,

parent, child,

Friends on earth,

and friends above;

For all gentle thoughts

and mild:

Lord of all,

to Thee we raise

This our hymn

of grateful praise.

For The Beauty Of The Earth

**Y**ou have given us not just precepts, but your devotion to each other, to your children, to your grandchildren, to others and, most of all, to the Lord, has been truly exemplary. We cannot thank you enough for the sacrifices you both made ... during the early years ... during the stormy passage of the early forties ... and later during times of peace at "Charis" in St Patrick's Road. We will never forget your thoughtfulness, advice and understanding, as we ourselves entered into marriage and then raised children with your love and devotion and sometimes leaving them entirely under your care ... We, your children and grandchildren ... call you both blessed." That was Dr Chew Chin Hin's tribute to Mum and Pop on behalf of the whole Chew family on the occasion of their Golden Anniversary Thanksgiving Dinner.

"Pop" — that was how the children addressed Dr Chew, except for the eldest, Chin Hin, who calls him "Pa," and Anna who calls him "father." How the American term came into use is a mystery to Dr Chew. It follows naturally that the grandchildren call him "grandpop." He has four children, although he will tell you that he has eight, because he considers his children's spouses as his own children. "I don't believe in in-laws. Someone once said that if you believe in in-laws they become outlaws." So he only has children and grandchildren, four of whom are married; and perhaps, some day, great grandchildren too — each one loved and warmly received into the Chew family.

Their eldest child, Cecil Chew Chin Hin was born at Hock Neo's parent's home a year after they were married. Next came Chew Chin Leong, born on 26 July 1933. Weighing ten pounds at birth, he was their most beautiful baby. A breech case, he died four days later, causing much grief to his parents. The church elders came round to the Chew's home, and one elder comforted them very much when he said, "God takes the fairest flowers into His garden." Dr Chew carried the little coffin himself to the Bidadari Cemetery, accompanied by the church elders, relatives and friends, whilst Hock Neo was still in bed recovering from the delivery. With the comfort that they had received from the Lord, the Chews were able to comfort many couples who suffered similarly. Two years later, Ruth Evelyn Chew Ai Lin was born at the Sepoy Lines Maternity Hospital. From the minute she was born she brought laughter and amusement to the Chew family. She was as bald as bald could be! "How can we have a girl without hair," exclaimed Dr Chew. But they had no cause for alarm; she eventually(after a year, that is) acquired a most luxuriant crop of hair. Just eleven days before Christmas of 1937, James Chew Chin Hian arrived. Dr Chew was listening to the BBC radio service and as the chimes of Big Ben came on the air, his telephone rang. As soon as he heard the good news he rushed off to the hospital. Their first three children were born in times of peace but when their last child, Ernest Chew Chin Tiong (known in the family as "Ernie") was born, their circumstances had changed drastically. Singapore was occupied by the Japanese forces and the Chew family was living in cramped and spartan quarters at the Yio Chu Kang Mental Hospital. Though times were difficult, their parent's trust in the sovereignty of God and their consistent love toward their children made for a secure and happy home atmosphere.

Dr Chew learnt from his mother the importance of disciplining children in love. On one occasion he failed to do this. He had come home after a hard day's work to find that four-year old Chin Hin had been up to some mischief. In anger, Dr Chew caned him. He immediately regretted his action, apologised to his son and gave him a hug. Ever since then he was careful to first determine whether his children's actions were pure mischief or naughtiness which is natural with children, or a moral misdeed. The latter called for correction but he would never discipline while he was still emotionally involved, and would first explain to the child why it was necessary to punish him.

The Chews recognised the uniqueness of each of their

children and never attempted to impress their mould on them. They were sensitive to and respected each one's special bent and encouraged him to pursue his interest. Chin Hin was inclined toward a medical career after witnessing the suffering of war casualties, a hospital mortuary packed with corpses, and his own father treating and comforting the wounded. Ai Lin was a bright girl who would be engrossed in a book for hours! She was best in reading, began writing poems early in life; and it was no surprise when she majored in English Literature at the University of Malaya in Singapore. Jim had the most stamina and was of a practical turn of mind. Quite naturally, he chose to read Economics. Ernest was the clear thinking and methodical one, and it was History that attracted him. Their father taught them that the Lord was in charge of their studies; He is sovereign over all knowledge and all human affairs. And that was the perspective with which they viewed not only their studies but all of life.

In a very real way, Dr Chew stood by each of his children and followed them through their education and career. When Chin Hin applied on his own to study medicine in Hong Kong, he paved the way for him by arranging for a Christian doctor friend, Dr H C Chan, to befriend him. It was there that Chin Hin met his future wife, Anna, his collegemate, and before they were married Dr and Mrs Chew went to Hong Kong to meet their future "daughter" and her family. Later, when Chin Hin went abroad for postgraduate studies with his wife for three years, Dr and Mrs Chew found much delight in looking after their eldest daughter, Elaine, and four-month old twins, Eileen and Eirene. Until his retirement from Government service in 1991, Dr Chin Hin was the Deputy Director of Medical Services for hospitals. Dr Anna was in the Department of Tuberculosis Control.

Having a Literature major in the house forced Dr Chew to shake the dust off his volumes of Shakespeare's plays and begin reading them all over again. He did not enjoy the Modern Poets; but for his daughter's sake, he studied them. Ai Lin graduated with honours, and the Christian public enjoyed many of her poems which were often featured in the IMPACT magazine where her father is chairman and regular contributor. Ai Lin is married to David Tan, later an elder of Bethesda Katong, and they are now residing in Tasmania.

The one who followed most Dr Chew's love of sports is Jim. He was into anything and everything in the way of extra curricular activities at school. As an athlete, he was best at middle distance running. Once, he wanted very much to take part in the 440-yard race at his school sports meet although he had a sprained ankle. Being the official doctor at the meet, Dr Chew examined his ankle, bandaged it, and gave him permission to run. Cheered on enthusiastically by his father, Jim came in a close second. Economics was far from being Dr Chew's favourite subject as he was disinclined to care about money; but when Jim decided to study Economics at the local university, Dr Chew girded himself up and carefully read through Adam Smith's "The Wealth of Nations." As they discussed the subject, Jim helped to balance out what Dr Chew calls "his silly ideas" about Economics. Recognising Jim's interest and potential in Christian service, his parents had been secretly praying for several years that their son would be a missionary. So it was a joyous moment for them when Jim announced that he would like to be a full-time Christian worker. He began as the Follow-up Director of Singapore Youth For Christ, and later joined the Navigators where he is now the Asia Facilitator serving from their New Zealand office. For some years Jim was Director of the Singapore Navigators. When he was training with the Navigators together with his wife, Selene, in the US and working in New Zealand, Dr and Mrs Chew expressed interest in what they were doing by visiting them in New Zealand. They later visited Glen Eyrie, the Navigators Headquarters in USA.

Ernest chose to read History at the University of Singapore and completed his Doctorate at St Catharines, Cambridge University. He acknowledged that it was his father who first helped him to think in historical terms by often talking to his children about their family history. Dr Chew read up enough history to be able to appreciate Ernest's theses for his Master's and Doctorate programmes. As with Chin Hin, when

Ernest was away for nine months at Harvard in the US for post-doctoral studies, and his wife, Aileen, joined him for four months, their two boys, Alistair and Emrys, were looked after by their grandparents. Associate Professor Ernest Chew later headed the History Department in the National University of Singapore (1983 – 1991) and is now Dean of the Faculty of Arts and Social Sciences. He is also an elder at Bethesda (Frankel Estate) Church and Chairman of the Graduates Christian Fellowship.

D r and Mrs Chew's life did not revolve just around their family. He firmly believes that a family should not be inward-looking. Both the Chews and their children were outgoing towards relatives and friends. When his younger brother Timothy died in 1952, his son Patrick joined the St Patrick's household. Theirs was an open home. When the children led their friends to the Lord, they would invite them to their home to meet their parents and they would inevitably be drawn into their family circle. One such friend is the Minister of National Development, Mr S Dhanabalan. He became a Christian during his school days through his classmate, Jim, who shared the Gospel with him. It was not long before he became part of the Chew family; Dr Chew became "Uncle Chew" to him and he was affectionately called "Bal" by his second family.

One reason for the security experienced by the Chew children was because their parents never disagreed in front of them; they aimed always to present a united front. One childhood incident of Dr Chew's may have led to this strong conviction. Once he witnessed his paternal grandfather in a fit of fury chasing his younger son with an axe. Dr Chew's mother rushed toward him and caught him around the legs and grabbed him tight till he calmed down. Terrified, Ben and his sister, Ada, were crouched in one corner of the room. That has made him deeply aware of the effect of violent disagreements on children and he did not want that to be the experience of his own children.

With two fine models of Christian living in the Chews', Christian teaching was more often caught than taught in the Chew home. The Chews lived out their life verse, "... seek ye first the kingdom of God, and His righteousness; and all these things shall be added unto you." Their whole life demonstrated the understanding that the Lord was in charge and He was always consulted. So the children grew up naturally understanding the sovereignty of God over all of their lives. Jim Chew describes it as the Deuteronomy 6 style of teaching; they talked to their children about God's ways "when they sit in their house, walk by the way, lie down and rise up..." Theirs was not a rigid home atmosphere; there was no forced family devotions. Occasionally, they would pray over a meal or just meet to pray. Some such times would be when they were facing a crisis in the family.

Mum Chew would in their early days tell the children Bible

stories; but as they grew up, each child was encouraged to
develop his or her own spiritual space. There was an element
of privacy in their spiritual growth. They read the Bible and
studied it for themselves, which is the practice of their own
father. They also learnt a lot from the Sunday School and
Bible Class at church. Jim and Ernest were in Dr Chew's class
at different times, and he taught them to relate the Word to
the world, giving exciting insights into the books of the Bible
and the meaning of verses. They were taught to approach the
Bible with the question: "What does it mean by what it says to
me and to my life?"

Spiritual truths were often related to life. Once Dr Chew
taught Jim a spiritual lesson in the course of his work.
Finding Jim awake in the early hours of the morning ,
he brought him along to make a house call. He drove
into a little lane in Changi and told Jim to wait in the car. He
returned and with a grave countenance explained to Jim that
he did what he could to save the patient but she died. "Jim,
there are some things that doctors can't do. We need to
depend completely on the Lord for our lives and for the
future." As they drove home in the quiet of the morning the
lesson came home to Jim that Christ was to be his
sufficiency, not his parents, teachers or anyone else. Another
special moment for Jim was sitting by the beach at their St
Patrick's Road home, looking across the sea at the
Indonesian isles during the Indonesian confrontation with

Singapore, and praying with his father for that neighbouring country — they being the only two who lasted through the all-night prayer meeting. History records the positive answer to their prayers and those of many others then. Dr Chew has an annexe in his room at "Charis" where he kept his stamp collections and prepared Bible studies and sermons. Sometimes, as a young boy, Ernest would find his way there to talk about stamps with him, and often the conversation would carry on to spiritual matters. The next generation also had occasion to learn spiritual lessons from Grandpop. Ernest's youngest child, Alethea, was one of them. When she was of kindergarten age, she would go to school by the schoolbus. However, one day she was adamant that her father drive her instead. When gently questioned by Grandpop, she confided: "A big boy punched me in the stomach."

"Is there any pain?" Dr Chew questioned further. When she answered no he continued, "Do you know why you were not hurt? It is because Jesus took care of you. He is with you wherever you go, so you don't have to be afraid."

She carefully thought through all that Grandpop said and replied, "But I can't see Jesus."

"Can you see the air around you?" asked Dr Chew. She shook her head. Then he wisely drew an analogy between Jesus and the invisible air. Assured of the reality of Jesus' presence and His protection, she went up the schoolbus the next day.

O n another occasion Alethea exclaimed, "The Government hates me." Surprised at her remark, Dr Chew questioned her and discovered what provoked it. She wanted very much to be enrolled in the Methodist Girls' School (MGS) but the Government policy then was not favourable toward the third child in the family, which she was. So she stood a slim chance of getting a place. Now that he understood her predicament, his advice to her was (the same as her parents!): "Alethea, why don't you pray and ask God to help you get into MGS if that is the place He wants for you." Her eyes lit up and she promptly made her request to God. When asked by her friends which school she was going to attend, she simply replied, "Why don't you ask God? He knows!" She did get into MGS, but more than that, she learnt about the sovereignty of God in her life.

Dr Chew believes that there are perils in being brought up in a rich home where a child can have everything he wants. His children were well provided for, but he did not indulge them. They restricted themselves so that they could give more to the Lord's work. All the Chew children experienced privation during the war years and the Japanese Occupation and it helped them to appreciate simplicity. As a family they led a quiet and simple life. Recreation was inexpensive — fishing, running, swimming, badminton, or a game of chess. They always managed to have a piano in the house. At times, Dr Chew would play a tune on the piano and that would be enough to start the family on a sing-song session. The love of music was something they all shared with their father.

All the children were brought up to know Jesus Christ for themselves. Conviction of sin and the saving knowledge of Christ's work on the cross — these are the work of the Holy Spirit alone, and for each of the Chew children He performed the miracle of salvation through the preaching of the Gospel at a church meeting. Chin Hin was baptised at age sixteen. Nine months later, both Ai Lin and Jim were saved through the preaching of J O Sanders. After that meeting, late at night, Dr Chew took them both for a long drive (knowing how much they enjoyed car rides) from Katong to the Gap at Pasir Panjang and then back to their home at Branksome Road. As he drove he talked with them about the Scriptures assuring them of their salvation in the Lord Jesus and encouraging them to grow as Christians. Jim was only ten then and Ai Lin was two years older. Ernest was about Ai Lin's age when he made a commitment to Christ. However, the real breakthrough in his spiritual life took place at a meeting when J O Sanders preached on Romans 6:1 ("What shall we say then? Shall we go on sinning so that grace may increase?"). He realised then that although he had earlier professed to have made a decision for Christ, there were many things in his life that were not right before God. Their involvement in the life of the church and in Christian service with other Christian organisations was a natural outflow of their commitment to Christ, throughout their youth and into adulthood.

Dr Chew sometimes jokingly calls Mrs Chew the "Minister for Home Affairs." If she is the "Minister for Home Affairs" then he must be the "Minister of Health," or simply put, the doctor in the house. He is always concerned for the health of his family, and this concern extended to his wife's family and his own aunts, sisters and their families. His own family had a fair share of sicknesses. When he was in his teens, Jim was rushed to the hospital when he complained of a sharp pain on his side. At two in the morning, he was operated on and his appendix was removed. When he ran a high fever after arriving in Penang for some speaking engagements, Dr Chew checked out Jim's symptoms over the telephone with Selene and suspected him as having infectious hepatitis. He ordered him to be sent back by the first plane and found that his diagnosis was correct. These and several other incidents were quite anxious moments for the Chews.

D r Chew's most anxious moment was when his wife fell seriously ill six days before their Golden Wedding Anniversary in 1980. Very early that Sunday morning, she was blue and practically pulseless. Dr Chew hurried her to hospital with the help of his eldest son, Dr Chin Hin. He prayed she would recover on the Wednesday for their Golden Anniversary celebration on Saturday. However, the thought that he might lose her still deeply troubled him.

Reluctantly, he had to leave her at the hospital that same
Sunday morning to speak at the wedding of two dear friends.
He arrived late and immediately after he finished speaking,
he made haste to return to her. When he learnt of the reason
for Dr Chew's haste, Bishop Chiu Ban It prayed with him
saying, "Lord, please heal Hock this very moment..." And he
knew that this was the right prayer and gave a hearty "Amen."
He confessed to God that his own prayer had partly depended
upon his medical knowledge. As they prayed together, he felt
peace and asked for forgiveness for his lack of surrender to
the Lord and for limiting Him.

When he reached the hospital he saw Hock Neo seated on
the bed, pink in the face with a normal blood pressure and
eager to go home!

"...We your children and grandchildren... call you both
blessed." As Chin Hin ended his tribute to his dear parents,
Dr Chew cast a glance at his beloved wife and thanked the
Lord that they could celebrate fifty years of their life together.
In many ways it was a celebration of the faithfulness and
loving kindness of God who has fashioned, guided and
blessed them and the generations after.

Ten years later, family, relatives and friends, each one
whose path in life at one point or more had crossed Dr
Chew's, each one whose life in body, mind or spirit, had been
touched by his, joined together with Benjamin Chew and
Hock Neo in thanksgiving to God for ten more years of His

grace in their life together. On this occasion of their Diamond
Wedding Anniversary Thanksgiving Dinner, Dr Chew, 83-year-
old patriarch, doctor, preacher, teacher, friend, with regard to
the future years chose these words of the Christian poet
Robert Browning:

"Grow old along with me!
The best is yet to be,
The last of life, for which the first was made:
Our times are in His hand
Who saith 'A whole I planned,
'Youth shows but half; trust God: see all nor be afraid! ' "

E P I L O G U E

Man of God

stubborn old war horse

Dr Luke now retired to become

Caleb of the mountains

      gently holding hands

      walking firmly comfortably

      with the wife of his youthful choice

      celebrating marriage adventure

      tried and joyous fifty five emerald years

      anticipating yet the best

with their Lord and God

Student of God

patient impatient vulnerable man

Dr Luke now retired to continue

meticulous philatelist

      touching exploring complex worlds

      enthusiast of classical music

      bemused by pop disco rock

      pianist extolling life in Bach

      Beethoven Chopin Schubert Mozart Handel's Messiah

      hymns of praise prayer passion

to his Lord and God

Servant of God

Mr Evangelical Singapore some say

Dr Luke now retired still serving

country church committee

      speaking at meeting discussing his wisdom Bible love

      well known yet not really known

      to people young middle-life old

      enjoying all including all

      child-like delight surprised by appreciation

      giving glory devotion

to his Lord and God

Child of God

Malacca-born patriarch of a tribe called Benjamin

Dr Luke now retired to remain

affectionately Pa father Pop

      grandfather gramps among progeny of varying ages

      stages of maturity immaturity

      amused proud exasperated always protecting

      seeing weariness building loving walls

      not suceeding sometimes not understanding

      his persistence strength beyond years, waiting

on their Lord and God

(This poem entitled "My Father" was written by Dr Chew's daughter, Tan Ai Lin for the Chews' 55th wedding anniversary in 1985).

As a young married couple we came into contact with Dr Benjamin Chew in 1958 through Youth For Christ in Singapore. We were then the only married couple amongst all the other youth.

Inspite being Pentecostal and he a Brethren, he encouraged us to be further committed in the Lord, and not long later we entered into theological studies for full-time ministry.

Since the 1970's we have had the pleasure of serving under his chairmanship in the Evangelical Fellowship of Singapore (EFOS) and two national rallies — The Billy Graham Crusade (1978) and the Luis Palau Mission (1986).

We have been greatly blessed by his personal prayer life and down-to-earth preaching of the Word.

Fred and Rita Abeysekera
Evangelists, Rural Ministry
Assemblies of God of Singapore

My friend, Dr Benjamin Chew is a gift to Christianity in Singapore. As a Methodist I take pride that his father was a lay pastor and teacher in the Methodist Mission and that Dr Ben's parents were brought together by Miss Sophia Blackmore of Singapore and Mrs E F Shellabear in Malacca. Although Dr Ben's ministry was in one church his leadership has by God's grace extended to all Protestant churches especially when it comes to evangelistic campaigns and mission strategies. His sterling character, his biblical knowledge and exposition and his graciousness to one and all make him all the more a model of a good Singaporean Christian gentleman and leader. I have often teased him that he was the archbishop of the church and he once said; "Don't get me into trouble with the Brethren". But the point is that no one else in our times has been able to get the co-operation of all Christians in Singapore when a cause needed a common mind and strategy. For this we should be thankful to God for such a blessing as Benjamin Chew.

Bishop Emeritus Dr T R Doraisamy
Archivist
Methodist Church in Singapore

Being Dr Chew's neighbour has been such a blessing from the Lord for our household. When we first moved next door to Dr Chew seven years ago we were not Christians and were not remotely interested in religion. We knew that Dr Chew and his family were staunch Christians so we tended to steer clear of them!

Three life-threatening crises in our home, however, forced us to turn to Dr Chew for help. Inspite of his busy schedule of meetings and talks all over Singapore, it was the Lord's mercy that at each of these emergencies, Dr Chew was home and able to quickly diagnose the problem and arrange for immediate treatment.

As we got to know Dr Chew and his family better, we sensed that, compared to them, there was something lacking in our family life. They came to know that we were hesitantly starting to search for the Lord, and as we found out later, they upheld us in their prayers.

One by one, our family came to know the Lord in our own time. Our maid, too, came to a saving knowledge of the Lord through her friendship with the Chews' maid. We thank God for the faithful witness of Dr Chew and his family. It helped to transform our lives.

Mr P Y Hwang & Mrs Polly Hwang
Deputy Chairman
Temasek Holdings (Pte) Ltd

In the past 15 years, I have had the joy and privilege of serving together with Dr Benjamin Chew in various Christian Committees. I am glad to have been acquainted with such a saintly and Godly man. He impressed me as a man who is deeply devoted to Christ and His work. There is such a fervency in his spirit for the expansion of God's kingdom. I am challenged by his commitment. Dr Chew's leadership is marked by humility and Christlikeness. Inspite of his great experience in the spiritual realm and in the medical arena, he does not have the air and pride that characterises many leaders. One feels comfortable in his presence. The beauty and fragrance of Christ permeates his life. I am encouraged by such leadership.

If Jesus tarries, and God wills for him to be here for many more years, I am sure his life will continue to touch many others.

Rev Dr Patrick Lau Kim Thiam
General Superintendent
Assemblies of God of Singapore

Being the eldest two in the family, with only two years difference between us, my brother and I were very close to one another. He was a very loving brother to me and his care extends to my own children. As children we shared a very large study table, and I would very often find him studying his Bible there instead of his schoolbooks. Bible study was a priority with him, even from his childhood days. As a doctor, his main concern was not to make a name for himself; his primary aim was to relieve the suffering of the sick. All through his life, in his quiet ways, he has helped many people. This was something that had been instilled in us since our childhood days. We were taught that the love of the Lord must be shared abroad in our hearts and this teaching has always governed his life.

Mrs Lee Keng Kiat (Ada Chew)

I first met Dr Benjamin Chew and his family in October 1953 at the Breaking of Bread Service in Bethesda Katong Church where he was (and still is) a beloved Elder. When I was appointed Dean at Singapore Bible College, I asked Dr Chew to come as our first visiting lecturer. From hence began a long association with that training facility. For several years we served together on the Singapore Keswick Committee.

He was a practising physician. Although he was a skilled practitioner, I do believe that medicine was his avocation. His first love and concern was to minister to the spiritual needs of people. A visit to his clinic in North Bridge Road would involve not only medication and counsel concerning health measures, but would always include a word of encouragement or admonition and pointed enquiry about each member of the family. Truly, he was one of the last of a noble order of "Family Doctors."

Benjamin is an honourable name, but when I think of Benjamin Chew's amazing contribution as both medical and spiritual doctor, I might suggest a middle name: Benjamin "LUKE" Chew. O, make that SAINT Luke!

Rev Dr Ernie Poulson
Senior Pastor
Grace Baptist Church

DR BENJAMIN CHEW AS I KNOW HIM...

Dr Benjamin Chew is a GENTLE WARRIOR of the Lord Jesus Christ. Totally dedicated to Him, he is a man of the Word, faithfully expounding it from pen and pulpit for the spiritual nourishment of students, professionals, church leaders and God's people generally. In his commitment to world evangelisation, both locally and cross-culturally, Dr Chew has played a leading and inspiring role in Singapore's national missions movement. He has a graciousness and breadth of spirit which has enabled him to give leadership to all evangelical groups. Despite his busy schedule, he is an exemplary and loving husband to his wife and father to his children in their Christ-centred home; a pastor of pastors; and a caring friend to those in pain. Most of all, Dr Ben is a true brother in Christ to me.

Dr James H Taylor III
Consulting Director For Chinese Ministries
Overseas Missionary Fellowship

Dr Chew's faithfulness and enthusiasm in his service to the Lord is an inspiration to us all. This is clearly evident in his life which is an open book to all; to quote Paul in 2 Corinthians 3:2: "an epistle known and read by all men."

Mr Lionel Ong
Elder
Bethesda (Frankel Estate) Church

I first came to know Dr Benjamin Chew as a young active Youth For Christ clubber in the mid-sixties. I had heard Dr Chew speak at several of our club meetings and was impressed by the clarity of his messages. Although a teenager then, I held him with high regard as I admired his abilities as a lay preacher and a committed churchman. In the last 19 years as a pastor, I have had many opportunities to meet up with Dr Chew. His positive spirit and his ability to make people feel at home in his presence has won him great admiration. It is no wonder that many regard him as an outstanding Christian leader in Singapore.

Dr Chew is now past 80 years of age, but he still remains fervent in the service of the Lord. He continues to preach boldly messages that the Lord has laid on his heart. I see in him a man who continues to reflect the beauty of Christ. He is a person worth emulating.

Rev Isaac Lim
Senior Pastor
Faith Methodist Church

My eldest brother, Benjamin is someone I not only love but whom I regard as a shining example of what a follower of Christ should be. He has often acted very much like our mother; self-sacrificing, and putting into practice what is learnt from the Bible.

One incident which touched me most about him was when our mother was very ill with ulcers. He must have felt very sad then but he would consider also the feelings of the younger ones. One night, I stared out of the window feeling lost. An arm went round me gently, and a voice said, "I will look after you should anything happen to mother." He was only a medical student; my father, my elder sister and brother were still around. But he cared most. How soothing the words were to my ears!

Mrs Lee Keng Yew (Annie Chew)

DR BENJAMIN CHEW AS I KNOW HIM...

The first time I heard Dr Chew was in the mid-fifties when he spoke to the Varsity Christian Fellowship. His topic was "Jesus Christ, the way, the truth and the life." His introductory remarks made a deep impression on me: Christ as the way — students in the arts faculty should welcome this theme for they are always trying to understand the ways of humankind through their studies of literature, history and philosophy. Christ as the truth — this should appeal to students of science for they are constantly trying to discover truths in nature. Christ as the life — this should strike a chord in the hearts of medical students whose whole training is directed towards the betterment of human life.

As I listened to Dr Chew, I realised that here was a man who not only loved God's word but also took pains to understand his audience. It is no wonder that so many people appreciated his teaching ministry.

Dr Bobby E K Sng
Secretary
Graduates' Christian Fellowship

I have known Dr Benjamin Chew for nearly 40 years. He is a leader and has been a father image in the Christian community. He is appointed as the permanent chaplain in the Gideons Camp because of his knowledge of the Bible. The members are much edified by his Bible exposition. He has a warm and wide heart to accept Christians from various denominations. Due to his exemplary life and knowledge of the Word of God he is appointed as advisor to many parachurch organisations.

Mr Goh Ewe Kheng
Elder
Church Of Singapore

A well known philosopher said that "The great use of one's life is computed not by its duration but by its donation." There are few whose lives have touched others both in duration and donation. Dr Chew is certainly one. Whenever I meet Doctor (as he is more affectionately known) I am reminded of his zest for life, his youthful sense of humour and his clarity of thought despite his age. Doctor served as the President on the Singapore Youth For Christ Board from its founding in 1957 till this year. His keen grasp of the changing environment around and his hectic schedule puts some of us serving with him and are half his age to shame. When he was approached to write his life story, Doctor was very reluctant. Only when he was satisfied that it will give glory to God was he persuaded to set aside time to do so. Readers, no matter what their ages are, will be challenged how a life lived for Him can bring joy and satisfaction for self and enrichment for others.

Mr Hia Chek Phang
Chairman
SYFC Board

I have known our beloved Dr Benjamin Chew for over thirty years. He has been and still is a wonderful friend, encourager, preacher, minister and a reference point to individuals and the Christian Community in Singapore and beyond. He well deserves the unofficial but affectionate designations –"Patriarch and Archbishop"!

The Rt Rev Dr Moses Tay
Bishop Of Singapore

To me, Dr Chew is a good example of the verse in 1 Corinthians 13 which says, "Love has no limits to its faith, its hope and its endurance." He has got a great capacity to trust people. He does not lose hope or faith in their good nature, although he knows from his Bible that man is a sinner. If a man has nine bad points about his character, and only one good point, he will choose to talk about that one good point. I do not think he is naive, nor is he one to compromise his principles. I recall one incident at an elders and deacons meeting where he firmly expressed that the church needs to be outgoing and not just look after itself in response to a remark that "charity begins at home." He raised his voice, thumped the table and said "Charity does not begin at home." He was prepared to stand his ground, but when it comes to judging people, he is very careful not to say anything that will hurt or damage them. These are the two things which I admire in him.

Mr S Dhanabalan
Minister Of National Development

I have known Dr Benjamin Chew since my returning to Singapore from Malaysia in 1977. I have always looked upon him as a fatherly figure, very patient, kind, and dedicated to the Lord. He has always struck me as a good Bible teacher. I thank God for his ecumenical contribution and leadership to the Singapore scene.

Bishop Ho Chee Sin
The Methodist Church in Singapore

GLOSSARY OF LOCAL TERMS

bungalow: large detached house

kapok: cotton used for stuffing pillows

kebaya: traditional costume of the Malay and Straits Chinese woman

lorong: side street or alley

masak-masak: playing house, often with toy cooking set

mosquito bus: small bus for a maximum of 8 passengers

padang: playing field

rotan: switch made of rattan meant for caning children

Senior Cambridge: major examinations taken at the end of the secondary school programme, set by a UK Board of Examiners

Straits Chinese: these were Chinese whose families had been resident in Singapore and Malacca for several hundred years and no longer spoke Chinese as their first language, but Malay. They had also adopted many Malay customs, particularly in manner of dress and food, but holding firmly to Buddhism

ABBREVIATIONS USED

BBC: British Broadcasting Corporation

BMA: British Military Administration

CIM: China Inland Mission

EFOS: Evangelical Fellowship of Singapore

CMO: Chief Medical Officer

MGS: Methodist Girls' School

OMF: Overseas Missionary Fellowship

PCMO: Principal Civil Medical Officer

SATA: Singapore Anti-Tuberculosis Association

TB: Tuberculosis

TTSH: Tan Tock Seng Hospital

YPG: Young People's Group

BIBLIOGRAPHY OF RESEARCH MATERIAL

1. *A Battle to be Remembered* Singapore: Oral History Department, 1988.

2. *Annual Report of the King Edward VII College of Medicine, Singapore,* 1929-1934.

3. *Annual Report of the Medical Department, Colony of Singapore,* 1946.

4. *Annual Report of the Tan Tock Seng's Hospital, Straits Settlements,* 1938.

5. *Bethesda Katong, 50 years and still growing,* Singapore: Bethesda Katong Church, 1986. Anniversary magazine published by the church.

6. *Calendar of the King Edward VII College of Medicine, Singapore,* 1925-1926

7. Chia, Felix, *The Babas* Singapore: Times Books International, 1980.

8. Da Silva, L.S., "Before and After Syonan-to. We left and Returned to General Hospital", *Singapore Medical Journal,* Vol. 26, 1985.

9. Dhanaraj, T.J., *Medical Education in Malaysia* Petaling Jaya: Pelanduk Publications (M) Sdn Bhd, 1988.

10. Doraisamy, Theodore R., *Forever Beginning – 100 Years of Methodism in Singapore,* The Methodist Church in Singapore, 1985.

11. Doraisamy, Theodore R., *Sophia Blackmore in Singapore* General Conference, Women's Society of Christian Service, 1987.

12. Doraisamy, Theodore R., *The March of Methodism – In Singapore and Malaysia 1885-1980.* Singapore: Methodist Book Room, 1982.

13. *Fifty Years of Medical Education in Malaya 1905-1955, Singapore* Singapore: The University of Malaya, 1955.

14. Haines, Harry J., *A History of the Methodist Church in Malaya* New Jersey: Princeton Theological Seminary, Princeton, New Jersey, 1956.

15. Ho Seng Ong, *Methodist Schools in Malaysia* Petaling Jaya Board of Education, Malaya Annual Conference, 1964.

16. *Journal of the Malayan Annual Conference,* 1909 & 1910.

17. Lau, Alfred, "The other side of the pulpit: Focus on the Tribe of Benjamin," Singapore: *Impact Magazine,* January 1977.

18. Means, Nathalie Toms, *Malaysia Mosaic – A Story of 50 Years of Methodism* Singapore: Methodist Book Room, 1935.

19. Lun, Vincent, *Dr Benjamin Chew: Doctor, Teacher and Servant of God* Singapore: Trinity Theological College, 1988.

20. Pearson, H.F., *Singapore: A Popular History 1819-1960* Singapore: Donald Moore for Eastern Universities Press Ltd Singapore, 1988.

21. Sng, Bobby, *In His Good Time - The Story of the Church in Singapore 1819-1978* Singapore: Graduates' Christian Fellowship, Singapore, 1980.

22. Song Ong Siang, *One Hundred Years' History of the Chinese in Singapore* London: John Murray, Albemarle Street, W. London, 1923.

LIST OF ILLUSTRATIONS

10. Bethesda (Katong) Church Sunday School in the late forties.

11. Post-war photograph of the Chews, year unknown.

12. A section of the crowd at the first evening of the Billy Graham Evangelistic Crusade in December 1978.

13. Dr Billy Graham preaching at the 1978 Crusade.

14. The Chews at their 50th wedding anniversary, 29 November 1980.

15. Geylang Police Station, 1905. Note the rickshaws on the right.

16. Early photograph of the Anglo-Chinese School. The school chapel is the building on the left.

17. Bras Basah Road, 1905. The site is presently occupied by the Cathay Cinema Building.

18. The Beach, 1910. A view of the beach along the East Coast, now reclaimed, perhaps not far from the runway of today's Changi Airport.

19. The jubilant victors who proclaimed themselves the "liberators" of Singapore when they took control on 16-February 1942.

20. The bombing during the Second World War destroyed many buildings. One such example, the Victoria Memorial Hall, is shown here.

21. Tanjong Katong, 1910. Along the sea one could find fanciful bungalows and more modest beach structures enjoyed by the well-to-do.

22. Local youths giving a rousing welcome to a foreign YFC mission team during the early years of Singapore Youth For Christ.